called to life

an invitation to a missional way of being

john c. hage
ellen creed branham

contents

words of gratitude

words of gratitude

We gratefully acknowledge the gifts of the multitudes who have helped this book evolve and come to fruition. For the participants who gave voice and thought to conversations in the missional life classes at Mt. Pleasant Presbyterian Church; for Trish Snead whom we would be lost without ; for Cheryl Glenn whose creativity energized the project through many generations and for Amy Heffernan who brought the project home; for Courtney Buxton whose attention to detail honed our writing; for our friends and families who encouraged and challenged us to step into the unknown; and always to our Creator God who sustains us through every aspect of work and to whom we give all honor and glory.

invitation

living a missional life is to be called to a new
way of being.

chapter 1:
Is there more?

"Our purpose in life is to discover meaning, and live according to it. We have therefore, something to live for. The process of living, of growing up, and becoming a person, is precisely the gradually increasing awareness of what that something is."[1]

"When we are pursued by the events in our lives to ask the gnawing questions about the meaning of it all, it is···God who has been stirring the questions in us. [Our] thirst is a gift from God who quenches the thirst."[2]

Do any of these stories sound familiar?

---

[1] Merton, Thomas. *No Man Is an Island*. New York: Harcourt, Brace, 1955. Print.

[2] Lindvall, Michael L. *A Geography of God: Exploring the Christian Journey*. Louisville, KY: Westminster John Knox, 2007. Print.

Michael is connected to his blackberry, which his wife has termed his "crackberry." He says he would love to be less distracted at home but feels, especially in this economy, if he does not keep up with work his employer will find someone who will. He often feel fragmented and pulled in so many directions.

Michael wonders...**Is there more to life?**

Sarah is a physician who got into medicine because she wanted to help people. Now, however, she finds herself fighting with her partners, and maximizing how many patients she can see in a day. She has given up looking to find meaning in what she does. Her focus, if she is honest is efficiency and getting through the day. On hard days she would love to give it all up.

Sarah wonders...**Is there more to life?**

Jess grew up in a Christian family and calls herself spiritual. Yet deep down she knows very little about what she believes. She generally thinks church is a building and a one hour Sunday service. She finds very little connection between that service and her work during the week.

Jess wonders...**Is there more to life?**

John remembers a sermon where the preacher asked, "Do you want titles or testimonies in your life?" The preacher asked the crowd, "Do you want more money, more stuff, more power or are you looking to live a meaningful life? A life filled with testimonies of grace, love, and service." John wonders how he can live that kind of life.

John wonders...**Is there more to life?**

Ellen, after a decade practicing architecture and, subsequently, nearly a decade of raising children, faces the realization that despite the innumerable joys of working and living, she longs for something "more." Not God, exactly, because it doesn't seem that God has gone missing. She feels a tug, a nudge, toward something else. But what? And who is pulling? She struggles to gain clarity regarding the work in the world to which God calls her. Ellen wonders... **Is there more to life?**

Is there more to life? Do you find yourself in any of these stories?

MANAGUA, NICARAGUA

We were gathered around a circle processing the day when one of the members of our mission team began to weep. She said, "I am successful. I graduated from the right school. I have a great job where I make more money than I need. But there has to be more to life. Is there more?"

What if, every once in a while, either in the simple routine of life or in moments outside of our comfort zone, we notice a whisper? A whisper deep down in our gut which says, "You were made for more..."

A CALL TO LIFE, AN INVITATION

This book is focused on encouraging you to listen to that whisper and follow where it leads. One assumption of this book is that God wants us to find life, meaning, and love. In fact, in the biblical scriptures of Isaiah 55, John 10, and John 14, God's call is to life. In Isaiah, the admonition is to "listen so that you may live" and in the Gospel of John, Jesus says that he has come so that we may have life and have it abundantly. What if it is true that God can offer us life? Would we listen? What if God offers that life to us in a whisper? Would we block out the other voices and listen to God's voice?

All of us experience meaningful moments through a whisper, nudge, or glimpse of abundant life.

Here are a few examples. Do any of these resonate with you?

MOMENTS OF TRANSCENDENCE
On an ordinary Wednesday, I (Ellen) recorded this beach experience. . .

The sky is thick with God this morning. Clouds hover, wind whispers, soundless rain and specks of built identity linger in the distance. The rays of the sun break through the endless horizontal with the confidence of the vertical, defining edges and outlining surfaces. This light—that is, illuminated power—stretches downward, caressing the earth. In this way, the splendid arms of God reach for us and we are held. Here, for a moment, for a walk, for all time, we have been visited by God—again. God creates a new day and it is good. Later, I see a humble white house punctuated in its middle by a bright yellow door. A feeling of rightness, of beauty, washes over me. I look ahead and see the line of the earth, held in place by trees and the way of things and I breathe in the holy glimpses we are given and I am reminded that I am to live life here, and partake in the abundance of this gift as best I can.

Often we are given glimpses in our lives that invite us to ask questions about God. There are moments which affirm that there must be something outside of ourselves. There are moments that beg the question, "Is there more?" Moments when you have looked upon the horizon and seen the sun setting over the ocean, or over the mountains, and have felt the awe of the natural landscape. Or, as you look at the intricate detail of a flower, the immensity of the blue whale, the curious waddle of a penguin, you have wondered, Is this particularity only about evolutionary usefulness or is there more?[3]   Perhaps you have encountered moments of an irrational love, which could not be explained through science.   Moments like a first kiss, birth of a child, or loss of parent where you have felt both the joy and pain of love which cannot be described with words or explained away through science.

MOMENTS OF MYSTIQUE

I have always been someone who is very germ conscious. I am forever washing my hands. My friends have always laughed my quirk. [On a mission trip,] I was playing with the children in Honduras, and a 10-12 year-old-boy with cerebral palsy came up to me. He was very crippled by it and could only mutter indistinguishable words; he drooled continually and wore unbelievably dirty clothes with a too small shirt worn inside out and backwards. His pants were falling off and he had not bathed in awhile. He came up to me and put his arms around me with his head against my chest; I was faced with a huge decision. The question was not 'Do I embrace this child?' but 'Can I embrace this child?' I immediately asked God to help me. I hugged him very tightly and rubbed his back. Holding him went on for several minutes, and I immediately thought of Jesus and the lepers. This nameless child was my encounter with Jesus and I could not hold back the tears.

There are instances in our lives when we feel called to risk as John's friend describes above or where we find ourselves equipped with a courage we didn't know existed within us.   When we move out of our unique comfort zones, we might find ourselves, sometimes surprisingly, immensely blessed.

---

[3] Rienstra, Debra. *So Much More: an Invitation to Christian Spirituality*. San Francisco: Jossey-Bass, 2005. Print.

Or perhaps we experience the unexplainable... A friend once described how he had been in a terrible car accident and remembered being moved from the car by a woman. In this act, he believes his life was spared. However, no one at the scene remembers seeing any woman. Is that just coincidence?

The beauty of our life as human beings is that we can feel. We can wonder, worry, and love; we can experience joy and pain. We can contemplate the mystery. We can ask about the back story. We can ask "Why?" or "Why not?" Choosing to ask questions might require courage on our part. It will require a willingness to pay attention and listen to the still voice within each of us. Are you willing to listen?

This book is founded upon the idea that if we are willing to listen and open our lives there is more and we can name it through a particular story: the story of a missional God. That there is a God who calls us to life and to a way of being in the world. An abundant life of meaning, hope, love, and grace.

The premise of this book is that we are called to life and we can experience real moments of goodness and love beyond ourselves. That our lives can be a part of a larger story of God's story. Our lives can be a part of a larger love, hope, and peace.

The reason we have written this book is because we have been given a gift. Through scripture, community and story we have come to see more clearly the life that God offers. We recognize that we cannot make it alone in the journey of life and so we encourage you to read this book with others (a trusted friend, a small group, a book club) to help identify the more you seek.

AN INVITATION TO THE MISSIONAL JOURNEY

Through stories found in scripture and in people who are living missional lives, we have encountered a set of common principles which include integrity, imagination, improvisation, incarnation, and inspiration. We see these as essential resources for navigation along the way and create space to see and live a missional life.

Integrity: We begin with questions that emerge from our own hearts and lives and explore them within the context of the missional life. We will consider questions such as: What do I believe about God and myself? Do I live out what I believe? How do I have hope while experiencing the reality of brokenness in my life and in the world? Can I be open to questioning personal as well as cultural assumptions ? Am I open to change?

Imagination:

One of the most powerful ways to experience this journey is to be open to a conversion of the imagination; to imagine a world through God's eyes. What would that be? Part of the growth in our imagination means that we examine the influence of culture in our lives. It also means that we imagine that God truly calls us to participate in God's work in the world. Do I believe it? How do I hear God call? And what does vocation have to do with it?

Improvisation:

We know that life in this world includes uncertainty. Often we look to the security of believing in a script for our lives. Yet, sometimes this tactic falls short and we are left wondering where we went wrong. In these chapters, we consider that, rather than a script, it is a story to which we are invited to contribute. We are invited to experiment and improvise, as well as to embrace an understanding of a kinship with all of God's world and the people who dwell in it. How can we release our fears and be open to the ongoing story?

Incarnation and inspiration:

The power of narrative is essential for the missional life. God's story of mission shapes our story here and now. In this section, we share stories of ordinary people who are living missional lives. From these stories, we hope to make some claims which reinforce the principles of the path and to inspire you to look for ways that you can live out your faith. We share stories not as models to emulate but because we seek to encourage you to compose your own life story. We believe sharing one's story is an essential part of life. We will also suggest additional resources for the journey to be continued beyond this book.

Playlist:

Any good trip needs great music. You will see that, at the end of each chapter, we have provided a song which may be helpful in thinking about the missional life. We encourage you to listen while you read. Let's go!

A FIRST STEP IN THE JOURNEY: LIVING IN THE TENSION

To start our journey we must first name the obstacles that cloud our vision. In order to be real about our circumstances and our world we must acknowledge the tension that we live in between how things should be and how they really are. Our conviction is that if we live with eyes wide open, we can see and experience a missional God even in the tension. For this is a God who calls us to life even in the difficult places.

Climb in. . .

So, welcome! We are glad and humbled that you have opened these pages. We hope you will feel an invitation to explore faith, meaning, and life. We hope you will find sanction to look deeply in your searching. Rather than answer questions, this book seeks to encourage you in the asking of the questions you carry upon your heart. As we begin this journey, we invite you to be willing to ask these questions of life and faith and to be open to transformation.

How can we find more? Let's keep going and see.

continue the conversation

1. Do any of these questions stir your soul? In the stories above, do you recognize any of these moments? If there is "more," can we name it?

> •Some of the first questions we ask of ourselves might be:
>
> •Is there something beyond myself?
>
> •How and where do I find meaning in my hectic life?
>
> •Why am I here? What is my purpose in life? Is this all just a cosmic accident?
>
> •What is the story of my life? What do I want it to be? What does a life well-lived look like?
>
> •Does God really call us? If so, what does that sound or feel like?
>
> •Are the relationships in my life meaningful?

2.   Have you ever experienced a moment of transcendence as described above? How did you see God working in that experience?

3.   Do you pay attention to the whisper, glimpses, or nudges that you feel? If so, how do you do that? If not, why not?

4. Do you empathize with the person in the beginning of the chapter who asked, "There has to be more to life?" Do you ever feel that way?   Do you ever feel trapped, bored, or lost? What is the "more" that you are searching for?

ideas for the road: pay attention

A friend once told me (John) that her favorite moment during Thanksgiving is when her mature aunt pulls her close as she is leaving the house and whispers, "I love you." Is this not what God does? Have you ever heard that whisper? In the midst of the busyness, take some time this week to listen. Pay attention to any whispers of love or moments of "more" and share the experience with someone.

playlist

"Hallelujahs", Deep Enough to Dream by Chris Rice

integrity

living a missional life is an opportunity to
look for God in moments of transcendence
and in the midst of tension. It is an
acceptance of God's invitation to the kingdom
here and now.

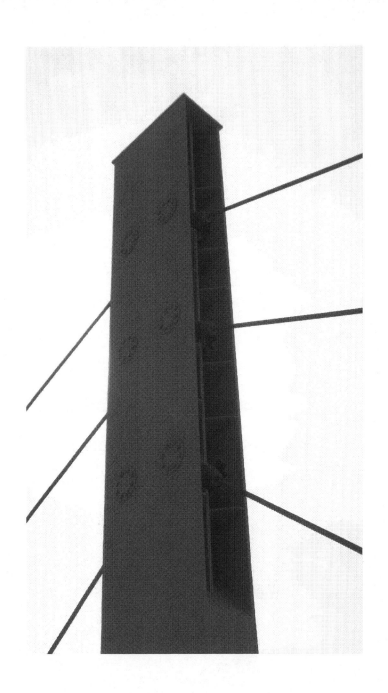

chapter 2:
living in the tension

"What humankind actually needs is not a tensionless state but rather the striving and struggling for some goal worthy of him. What he needs is not the discharge of tension at any cost, but the call of meaning.[4]

"Welcome to the planet...the tension is here
Between who you are and who you could be
Between how it is and how it should be."

These words, from the song "Dare You to Move" by the popular rock band Switchfoot, seem to sum up the tension many of us feel in our lives. The tension between unmet expectations of who we are and the dreams of who we could be. The tension between the reality of violence and pain and the vision of love and peace. The

---

[4] Frankl, Viktor Emil. *Man's Search for Meaning*. New York: Washington Square, 1984. Print.

tension between how we live and what we believe. The tension between the reality of our fragmented, hyper-busy lives and the search for a cohesive life which points to something larger than our do-list for the day. In small or large ways, do you experience these tensions? If so, how do we keep it together in the face of this reality?

Part of living a missional life is to recognize these tensions. We must first name the water that we enter before we know in what direction we should swim. What if Switchfoot's lyrics make a great point? Recognizing the reality of tension is the first step in exploring the direction of our lives. When we name the tension in which we all live, we can better understand the nature of God's movement in us and in the world.

TENSION: EVEN IN SCRIPTURE

Jesus called them over to him and began to speak in parables..."If a house is divided against itself, that house cannot stand." (Mark 3:23-25, selected, NIV)

Taking the five loaves and the two fish and looking up to heaven, [Jesus] gave thanks and broke the loaves. Then he gave them to his disciples to distribute to the people. He also divided the two fish among them all. They all ate and were satisfied. (Mark 6:41-42, NIV)

Even here, in scripture, we see tension in place. To be divided against self is not life-giving, but to bless and break and divide for all is a gift. To be divided against self is, perhaps, to ignore the blessing of being divided, being pulled in seemingly opposing directions. To ignore the pulling-ness, and to turn away is to miss the blessing of being in the miracle.

TENSION: THE NECESSITY OF IT

Consider a building, perhaps a high-rise made of steel and glass, which soars beyond our immediate vision. Or consider a humble dwelling, a stable even, with sturdy walls and a protective roof against the elements. The two structures have a common value which is tension. Without the pulling force of tension impregnated within the very character of the construction materials, each of these buildings would fail. A structure of human making cannot stand without the presence of the tensile force.

It is our belief that by naming, recognizing, and living into these tensions, the life of faith can stand over a lifetime and we can even find God at work. This recognition is important because it creates space in the life of faith to name the reality of a loving God while also acknowledging the mystery and questions of life. Naming these tensions will not create weakness but, as in a building, will provide strength.

TENSION: EVEN IN JESUS?

In the missional life, tension may be experienced through forces that pull away from, or seem to oppose, each other. These forces may also be identified as dualities because they appear as "two sides of the same coin." Some of the concrete dualities that exist in the missional life are presented below.

Human/Divine

First, we find an inherent tension within our confession that God is fully human and fully divine. In the Gospel of John, chapter 1, it is written:

> *"In the beginning was the Word, and the Word was with God, and the Word was God. . . the Word became flesh and made his dwelling among us. . ."*

We confess that God in the person of Jesus lived among us, being human, yet also being divine. From this understanding, we wrestle with our response. We perceive other dualities that exist in tension in the missional life, including:

Law/Grace, Truth/Mercy, Mind/Heart:
Can forgiveness trump law? Can the guilty go unpunished? Can my heart convince my head to infuse knowledge with love? These questions are raised in the context of a missional life. By Jesus' own example, we see a person who knew and valued the Law and who responded from the heart with mercy and love.

Finite/Infinite:
Created in God's image, we are infinite beings caught in finite time. Our doings, our goings, and our works subscribe to a finite system of interaction. Yet we believe in an infinite God, and thus our hearts and our minds and our souls are set to the song of God's time. Our life on earth must continually traverse the threshold between these realities.

Friday/Sunday:
The darkness of the Friday night in Gethsemane, the violence of the cross, the ignorance of the people—we are here. We see ourselves in the mob, in the shouts, in the pale words of Pilate, and in the judgment. Yet. Sunday comes. We are here, too. We gasp at the empty grave. We rub our eyes in disbelief in the presence of the resurrected Lord. With Mary, we confess that we have seen him.

Conviction/Uncertainty:
We know what we have been taught to believe, and sometimes we believe it. We are certain of God's love for us, yet we act against one another, seemingly under the assumption that God's love is portioned out in unequal amounts after all. We believe we are saved but we

work tirelessly to prove ourselves to God. Perhaps we are not sure of our salvation because the path is just too mysterious. We are uncertain of ourselves and our place in the world. We wonder when we are faithful yet hear only God's silence.

Doing/Being, Acting/Waiting, Achieve/Receive:
These three share certain similarities.   In some ways, perhaps the missional journey is most concerned with these. We are called to BE like Christ and to DO God's will.   We feel the need to respond to so many needs around us and yet we feel used up and perhaps decidedly un-Christ-like at the end of the day. We hear God tell us to be still and let God be God and yet we know God has instructed us to feed the poor and minister to the broken. We strive to achieve in order to prove ourselves worthy and yet we forget to receive the abundant grace Christ offers us at the point of utter unworthiness.

THE IN-BETWEEN PLACE
What is it about the force of tension in our lives that may cause us to look askance, to try to find a way out? Do we settle for one "side" or the other, rather than dwell in the midst of these opposing forces?

The dualities which appear to oppose, which pull away from one another, create an in-between place.   This holding of two opposites in tension is honest. It creates an openness, a faith that waits and sees. A faith based on, well, faith. A faith in things not fully seen, but seen. A faith in things not fully understood and yet understood. A faith based on trust in a God, who cannot be defined by the limits of human reason but came in the particular form of Jesus Christ. This in-between place is the place of growth, discernment, and honesty. Are you willing to live there, in that liminal space?

CHRIST: CONVEYOR OF THE LIMINAL

Merriam-Webster Dictionary defines liminal as: "Of, or relating to, or being an intermediate state, phase or condition; IN-BETWEEN, transitional. Origin from the Latin word meaning threshold." (emphasis added)

Joseph took the body [of Jesus], wrapped it in a clean linen cloth, and placed it in his own new tomb that he had cut out of the rock. He rolled a big stone in front of the entrance and went away." (Matthew 27:59-61)

WHAT OF SATURDAY?

This brief passage from the account of Jesus' death and resurrection provides a wonderful metaphor for the liminal space. Joseph takes Jesus' body. He wraps it in a clean cloth and places it in a new tomb. So often we find ourselves in such an in-between place and it is indeed new. It doesn't feel like what we're used to; it doesn't feel like what we know. And, even if the life we know is dusty, tiresome, or barren, we're not so sure about the clean new place where we find ourselves.

Then Joseph rolls a large stone to cover the door of the tomb and he leaves. Mary Magdalene and the other Mary are waiting, outside, sitting opposite the tomb. When we're in the tomb and the stone has been rolled over its opening, blocking out light, blocking our vision to see beyond our immediate boundary, we don't see those who are waiting for us. We don't see those who are holding hope for us. Even if they don't know how it will happen, they are waiting and believing for us, believing that it will happen. Such is the community of faith; this believing joins and informs the individual journey within the community of believers.

From the scripture passage we know that on Saturday before the resurrection, they made sure the tomb was secure. Yet we don't glean much about what exactly happens on that day. Isn't that too like our life? Sometimes when we emerge from the liminal space, when God has breathed new life into us again, we may not be able to explain exactly what happened. Still, we know that our life has changed and we know that it wasn't through our own power, but through God's.

Another way to consider the liminal experience is the womb. As an expectant parent can attest, waiting for a child to be born, the womb is surely a liminal space. Perhaps the medical community has provided a "due date" and perhaps the birth will happen in accordance with our plans – or, perhaps not—but we believe it will happen.   Then life will surely be different than on the other side of the womb, before the womb was filled with emerging life.

Likewise, in the liminal space we know that life is sure to change but we don't know how. We often don't have the vision or the imagination to see how but if we let ourselves participate in that space; if we let ourselves be consoled by the walls of the new tomb and the security of the rock; if we allow ourselves to remember that there are others waiting for us, then we open ourselves to seeing God at work in the tomb. Not magic… but rather an unfolding of God's divine plan, an unfolding of what is to be even if we don't know what that is.

The liminal dimension bridges the gap between the tensions we see in our lives. The tension is not merely a line between opposites, but an intentional place where something happens. Instead of choosing one or other, we can, with courage, stay awhile in the place of mystery. We can exist, and grow, upon holy ground, in this middle place, this threshold and expect to meet God. Being attentive to perceived dichotomies fosters the missional life by allowing one to accept the significance of both "sides," and to therefore live in a place defined by apparent opposites where one hears and responds.

We are to be both disciple (follower) and apostle (one who is sent out). Jesus is the one whom we follow and who sends us out and in whom the following and going-out can make sense together. The paradox is made clear in Christ whom we emulate and in whose mission we participate. In Christ, where mercy and truth have met.

WHAT THEN?

What does this mean for the individual? Claiming God's help, we seek the courage to live in the liminal space, where answers do not come easily and where decisions can torment the soul, but where the peace of God beyond our understanding makes its claim. We hope to find where true life is lived and where the divine is encountered. That is, to borrow from Frederick Buechner, the place where one's "deep gladness" intersects the "deep need" of the immediate world, as a pin must puncture fabric in two points, cradling the cloth between.[5]

What does this mean for the church in society? Christ, as the conveyor of the liminal, encourages us to seek an understanding of the gospel as both personally compelling and socially instructive. The balance of our lives is drawn to a place of equilibrium, a liminal place perhaps, where we meet Christ. Such a life may be difficult in our society. Perhaps we are afraid of living in a place where dualities co-exist; a place where neither portion is realized to its own completion and there is no clear answer. Are we afraid because it's messy? Because our selves are revealed and changed as well? Because it means to live, at least somewhat, in the unknown? To live here

---

[5] Buechner, Frederick. *Wishfull Thinking: A Theological ABC*. New York:Harper & Row, 1973. Print.

means to accept the limits of our own understanding and to lean into the mystery of God and community.

Do we sometimes miss the bigger picture? Accepting our limits is instructive for appreciating the sovereignty of God and being pointed toward the great joy of relationship. Then we may experience the joy of collaboration. When one's gift complements another's gift and the two are added to the gifts of others in community, suddenly our realm of understanding and experience is expanded multifold and our inner depths are fed. This nourishment of the soul does not happen when one is isolated in an ivory tower of self-righteous opinion, or when we are afraid to "leave the church," but occurs in the liminal place. Perhaps the liminal place is rather like soil—where ideas and actions provide the compost for new growth; where belief and behavior are broken down and changed and the evolved result is pronounced good.

INVITATION TO A DEEPER FAITH

What do we do with the tension in our lives? Perhaps the tension is an invitation to a deeper faith; an invitation to accept the pull of incongruous sides, to accept the unexplainable, and to agree to be in this in-between place. Maybe this is not a place to escape but one in which to experience God, and to grow. So to meet God, we consider that to embrace "both-and" is to keep our heart open to seemingly opposite truths. We shrug off the either/or, the sense of false security in professing one certainty over another. Perhaps, then, we are open to see God at work. Perhaps by choosing to live in the midst of these dualities, we can catch a glimpse of the abundant life Christ promised.

continue the conversation

1. Can you name the tensions in your life? Can God

work in those tensions?

2. Do you think naming, recognizing, or living in the tension can create space for growth? Would it free you in any way to "move" in a new direction?

3. Do you ever feel as if you are in a liminal space, that in-between place? Do you think God can create there? How do you feel about going into the liminal space, where answers do not come easily? Are you comfortable with some mystery in your faith?

ideas for the road: a story

A friend of John's was struggling through cancer when she wrote this note. It is a powerful reminder of living in the tension of life and death and seeing God even in that place. Maybe her story will encourage you to keep looking for God as well.

I've lost my hair so it's scarves and hats and wig...doesn't feel natural at all. I feel like there's a helmet on my head. I picked a short style which looked less "wiggy." Those who have seen it say it's great. I say it's ok... better than bald. It IS something to loose your hair within a week's time.

You've probably noticed that Linda's name appears regularly when I write. All my kids have been so supportive and loving. Jim calls almost everyday. He's coming again to visit in August. This time Jill will be with him and I am really looking forward to seeing them both. Linda has been off for the last month so she has really knocked herself out for me. The rewards of this cancer as far as my relationship with my kids go far surpass the negatives of the disease. I feel loved by them and so many of you out there!

God has a plan here, my friends. I don't know what it is in total but I feel His presence. The phrase that keeps coming back is," there is peace with praise." That's a phrase that was given to me when I had my mastectomy 16+ years ago. It comes to me when I am most down. If I can get myself out of myself and I simply praise God and think of all my blessings, peace is there. Just another gift given. Whether I am going to lick this thing or not, I know I am healing.

I do so appreciate all your care. Thank you for not leaving me through all of this. Your thoughts, prayers, phone calls, emails, cards, visits, food, wig trips, and rides mean so much. Thanks team.

Love to you all,
Cindy

playlist

"Dare You to Move", The Best Yet by Switchfoot

You are in this time of the interim
Where everything seems withheld.

The path you took to get here has washed out;
The way forward is still concealed from you.

As far as you can, hold your confidence.
Do not allow your confusion to squander
This call which is loosening
Your roots in false ground,
That you might come free
From all that you have outgrown.[6]

---

[6] John O'Donohue, *For the Interim Time*

chapter 3:
a missional God

"The journey of faith is not so much to 'find God' as it is a struggle to follow a God who finds us."[7]

"So if anyone is in Christ, there is a new creation: everything old has passed away; see, everything has become new! All this is from God, who reconciled us to himself through Christ, and has given us the ministry of reconciliation; that is, in Christ God was reconciling the world to himself, not counting their trespasses against them, and entrusting the message of reconciliation to us. So we are ambassadors for Christ, since God is making his appeal through us. We implore you on Christ's behalf: be reconciled to God." (2 Corinthians 5: 17-20)

---

[7] Lindvall, Michael L. *A Geography of God: Exploring the Christian Journey*. Louisville, KY: Westminster John Knox,2007. Print.

HOW ARE THINGS SUPPOSED TO BE?

What kind of God can exist in the tension of life? Is this a God you can believe in?

In the movie *Grand Canyon*, a tow-truck operator played by Danny Glover, tries to help a motorist who is stranded with a flat tire. While the motorist, played by Kevin Kline, is waiting, he is approached by a gang. They intend to take his car and money, and beat him up. In an exchange with the gang the tow-truck operator says, "This is not the way things are supposed to be."

Don't we all feel, at some point, that something is wrong? We feel that things are not the way they are supposed to be. For Christians, this is the reality of brokenness or separation from God; the realization of sin which separates us from our brothers and sisters and from God. This is the tension that we live in: the way the world should be and how it is.

BEYOND "HEAD TRIP" TO WAY OF LIFE

John Calvin, a reformed theologian, begins his work, *Institutes of the Christian Religion* by saying that there is no true knowledge of self without knowledge of God. If Calvin is right, what kind of God do you believe in?[8]

One of my frustrations early on with faith was that I (John) grew up in a Christian family and attended a great church and yet, many times I wondered, is this all just a head trip? Is God just an intellectual framework? Does faith actually move people to action? Is God really alive?

A MISSIONAL GOD

If we read scripture carefully and if we open our eyes, we can know and experience a missional God. This missional God should profoundly shape our identities as in-

---

[8] Calvin, Jean. *Institutes of the Christian Religion.* Philadelphia: Westminster, 1960. Print.

dividuals and as a church.

As individuals, it should form who we are by shaping our goals, our aims, and our purpose in life. If our theological understanding of God is missional, our identity should be shaped by that understanding. We believe in a missionary God who is alive and at work in this world—a God who invites us to be a part of God's reconciling mission in the world. This belief should construct the lens by which we understand our aims, goals, and purpose in life. It should also shape how we live, how we worship, and how we understand the church, and salvation.

Let's unpack what it means to proclaim a "missional God" by looking at three aspects: Kingdom of God, Incarnation, and Trinity.

THE KINGDOM OF GOD

What do you believe about God? Is God alive and at work in the world? Many Christians would say, "Yes, God is at work in the world but we just don't know how."

Let's ask this question in another way: do you think that after God formed the world, God completed all creative activity in our lives? Do you believe in a "watchmaker" God who, in designing the world, wound it up as a watchmaker and then withdrew?[9]

In scripture, a recurring Gospel message is that the Kingdom of God is at hand. Both John the Baptist and Jesus proclaimed the nearness of God's kingdom (Matthew 3:2; 4:17; Mark 1:15). Without the lens of faith, can we see Christ's kingdom? Can we see God at work?

---

[9] Frost, Michael. *Seeing God in the Ordinary: a Theology of the Everyday*. Peabody, MA: Hendrickson, 2000. Print.

AN INCARNATIONAL GOD

A key passage for a missional people to gain an understanding of a missional God is a story Jesus told his disciples:

> *Then the king will say to those at his right hand, "Come, you that are blessed by my Father, inherit the kingdom prepared for you from the foundation of the world; for I was hungry and you gave me food, I was thirsty and you gave me something to drink, I was a stranger and you welcomed me, I was naked and you gave me clothing, I was sick and you took care of me, I was in prison and you visited me." Then the righteous will answer him, "Lord, **when was it that we saw you** hungry and gave you food, or thirsty and gave you something to drink? **And when was it that we saw you** a stranger and welcomed you, or naked and gave you clothing? **And when was it that we saw you** sick or in prison and visited you?" And the king will answer them, "Truly I tell you, just as you did it to one of the least of these who are members of my family, you did it to me." (Matthew 25:34-40, emphasis added)*

"Lord, when did we see you?" That question is so honest. This is often our question. Where do we see God at work?

The promise of the missional life is that we can see God at work. We can see Christ in the hungry, in the sick, and in those who are in prison. We can see Christ and the Kingdom of God wherever peace, joy, love, and mercy reign. This is the in-breaking of the Kingdom. This is what Christ came to proclaim and this reality is here and now. The promise is that our eyes can be opened to see God at work just like the disciples on an ordinary journey.

The Gospel of Luke tells a story which occurred just after the crucifixion of Jesus. As the disciples walk along the road toward Emmaus, accompanied by a stranger, their eyes are opened…

Now on that same day two of them were going to a village called Emmaus, about seven miles from Jerusalem, and talking with each other about all these things that had happened. While they were talking and discussing, Jesus himself came near and went with them, but their eyes were kept from recognizing him. And he said to them, 'What are you discussing with each other while you walk along?' They stood still, looking sad. Then one of them, whose name was Cleopas, answered him, 'Are you the only stranger in Jerusalem who does not know the things that have taken place there in these days?' He asked them, 'What things?' They replied, 'The things about Jesus of Nazareth, who was a prophet mighty in deed and word before God and all the people, and how our chief priests and leaders handed him over to be condemned to death and crucified him. But we had hoped that he was the one to redeem Israel. Yes, and besides all this, it is now the third day since these things took place. Moreover, some women of our group astounded us. They were at the tomb early this morning, and when they did not find his body there, they came back and told us that they had indeed seen a vision of angels who said that he was alive. Some of those who were with us went to the tomb and found it just as the women had said; but they did not see him.' Then he said to them, 'Oh, how foolish you are, and how slow of heart to believe all that the prophets have declared! Was it not necessary that the Messiah should suffer these things and then enter into his glory?' Then beginning with Moses and all the prophets, he interpreted to them the things about himself in all the scriptures.

As they came near the village to which they were going, he walked ahead as if he were going on. But they urged him strongly, saying, 'Stay with us, because it is almost evening and the day is now nearly over.' So he went in to stay with them. When he was at the table with them, he took bread, blessed and broke it, and gave it to them. **Then their eyes were opened, and they recognized him;** *and he vanished from their sight. (Luke 24:13-31, emphasis added)*

Then their eyes were opened and they recognized him...
Every once in a while, on an ordinary road, our eyes can be opened to God's kingdom and we recognize him. One of the unique themes of the Christian story is that God, the creator of the universe, came to us in the form of a child. This is the incarnation. What is even more radical is that this God came, not as a dominating King, but in the form of a servant. God became incarnate in Christ in order to embody true love and to reconcile God's creation (Philippians 2).

At the heart of a missional life is the belief in an incarnational God. It opens our eyes not to a dead god but to a living God. It opens our eyes not to a deistic god but to a God at work all around us and in us. It opens our eyes not to an agnostic god but to a God we can know. And yet, this story begins even before the incarnation of Christ with the triune nature of God; that is, the Trinity.

TRINITY AND SENDING
One of the often ignored theological ideas of the Christian faith is belief in the Trinity. This is the idea that God is three-in-one. Because this idea is hard to explain, it is frequently sidelined in favor of other theological constructs (justification, salvation, etc.). But the Trinity is

central for understanding the missional perspective as a pattern of calling and sending. In this pattern, we get a view of the heart of God and a picture of the relationships between Father, Son, and Holy Spirit. With an understanding of the Trinity, we can receive the gift that our lives are a part of a larger story. Our lives are a part of God's long story of sending, beginning with God's self. David Bosch, a contemporary theologian, says it this way:

> Mission is understood as being derived from the very nature of God....The classical doctrine of the missio Dei as God the Father sending the Son, and God the Father and the Son sending the Spirit is expanded to include yet another "movement"; Father, Son and Holy Spirit sending the church into the world. [10]

This concept helps us to consider that mission is not a program added to our religion but is intimately and deeply intertwined in the very nature of God. Part of what it means to be missional is that we believe what Jesus said, "As you have sent me into the world, so I have sent them into the world." (John 17:18, emphasis added). We understand ourselves as being a sent people who are called to a mission of reconciliation. We are invited into bringing about God's kingdom. This is our larger mission and this is where we can find meaning in our lives as Christians.

If we take a missional view of the Christian story, God's kingdom is where God is at work. Wherever there is peace, love, joy, justice, mercy, and faith, we get to see glimpses of God's kingdom. If we believe in a creative and incarnational God, then we believe that God is creating all around us and in us.

---

[10] Bosch, David Jacobus. *Transforming Mission: Paradigm Shifts in Theology of Mission*. Maryknoll, NY: Orbis, 1991. Print.

THE REALITY OF A BROKEN WORLD

Do we see Christ all the time or do we only get glimpses? In 1 Corinthians 13:12, Paul writes, "Now we see but a poor reflection as in a mirror; then we shall see face to face. Now I know in part; then I shall know fully, even as I am fully known." We don't see fully due to sin which distorts our vision and blurs God's work in the world.

Why doesn't God just waive a magic wand to fill the world with love and end violence? While we will never fully answer this question, Australian theologian Michael Frost believes that God does not act in this way "because God prefers to dignify us by inviting us to be partners in creating love and being a part of the extension of God's kingdom." [11] Frost's point for us is to understand that God loves in freedom. God does not force us to live in certain ways but invites us to true life and even, through free will, allows us to turn away. What if we choose to turn towards God? What if when we turn to be a part of God's reconciling work in the world, we accept an invitation to salvation, not just in heaven, but here and now? We accept an invitation to life where we can experience deep meaning and hope.

A HOLISTIC UNDERSTANDING OF SALVATION

A missional understanding of God shapes our faith so that we understand that we are invited to participate in God's mission of reconciling the world. The primary goal is not personal or individualistic salvation attained at the end of our life. That is a reductionism of the true breadth and depth of the gospel. What we are offered in Jesus Christ is abundant life here and now. Yes, we do believe in the promise of eternal life, but we are offered purpose and mission here and now.

---

[11] Frost, Michael. *Seeing God in the Ordinary: a Theology of the Everyday*. Peabody, MA: Hendrickson, 2000. Print.

British Theologian N.T. Wright explains it this way:

The work of salvation, in its full sense, is (1) about whole human beings, not merely souls; (2) about the present, not simply the future; and (3) about what God does through us, not merely what God does in and for us. If we can get this straight, we will rediscover the historic for the full-orbed mission of the church. . . [A] proper grasp of the future hope held out to us in Jesus Christ leads directly and, to many people, equally surprising, to a vision of the present hope that is the basis of all Christian mission. To hope for a better future in this world—for the poor, the sick, the lonely, and depressed, for the slaves, the refugees, the hungry and homeless, the abused, the paranoid, the downtrodden and despairing, and in fact for the whole wide, wonderful, and wounded world—is not something else, something extra, something tacked on to the gospel as an afterthought. And to work for that intermediate hope, the surprising hope that comes forward from God's ultimate future into God's urgent present is not a distraction from the task of mission and evangelism in the present. It is a central, essential, vital and life-giving part of it.[12]

THE NEED FOR ONE ANOTHER

A missional life is one where we believe that God is alive, and that we are called and sent to be a part of a larger mission, God's mission. We understand the invitation to this mission as a gift of salvation, a radical summons to life that is not forced, but given freely by God. Will we accept it? How do we embrace it?

---

[12] Wright, N. T. *Surprised by Hope: Rethinking Heaven, the Resurrection, and the Mission of the Church*. New York: HarperOne, 2008. Print.

In our reformed tradition, we confess our tendency to turn inward and focus on ourselves. We recognize our inclination to choose what is easy and most rewarding. The veracity of this assertion leads us to confess that we need each other as the body of Christ. Along the journey, we need to encourage, support, and challenge each other not to turn inward, but to take risks and participate in God's mission by looking outward. To accept God's invitation, we depend upon the presence of the community of faith because we will be asked to take steps which are countercultural. Steps which are risky. Steps based upon faith.

INTEGRITY AND THE MISSIONAL CONVERSATION
A key step for me (John) in my journey of faith has been being part of the missional conversation. It has allowed me to make connections that were missing in my faith. It has helped me integrate faith and action, not as separate camps fighting for truth, but as an integrated whole in a Trinitarian God. It has helped me see my life as being integral to a larger mission, God's mission. It has helped me connect Sunday worship to Monday work and vice versa.

Missional theology not only names the reality of God, but it gives us a way to hold it all together with integrity as we face ever more fragmented lives. It also challenges us to integrate what we believe with how we live. In many ways, missional theology breaks down the box that many of us have put God in and challenges us to open our eyes to God around us and in us.

BEING ACCOMPANIED DOWN THE ROAD
Our hope, founded in the promise of a missional God, is that—if we are discerning, looking, praying, and stepping out in faith—we can take part in God's mission. Can you take a step of faith, trusting in a missional God? To go

that distance, we are called to a new way of seeing, hearing and responding. Looking for portals in our lives through which we experience the presence of God, we are called to a sacred, prophetic, missional imagination. We are called to listen for a still small voice amidst the voices of the world, and we are called to have an improvisational response. We embrace the freedom that is offered in the resurrection and trust in the promises of a living God. Are you willing to do that? If so, let's continue down the road.

continue the conversation

1. Does believing in a missionary God affect your life? Would this change how you live? Why or why not?

2. Is this broader or nuanced understanding of the Trinity, the Kingdom of God, or salvation helpful to you in your journey of faith? Are these new concepts for you? Does this change how you would live? Why or why not?

3. Do you believe in an Incarnational God? Do you think we can actually see God at work? Do you think we can experience God's Kingdom?

4. If you consider yourself a Christian, have you ever found yourself complacent in your belief of personal salvation, forgetting to search for purpose and mission here and now?

ideas for the road:
opportunity in the ordinary

Everyday we find ourselves on an ordinary road. It may

be around the water cooler, in the grocery store, or on a local walking trail. What if these places could be portals to the in-breaking of God's kingdom here and now? The next time you find yourself in such a place, look into the eyes of a stranger in your midst and consider that it could be the Christ. Let yourself be renewed by this interaction. Pray for this person and be open to how God may be calling you to respond.

playlist

"I Saw God Today", <u>Now That's What I Call Country</u> by George Strait

imagination

living a missional life is to be aware of
cultural forces which shape identity while at
the same listening for God's call to life
abundant.

chapter 4:
renewing our minds

Therefore, I urge you, brothers, in view of God's mercy, to offer your bodies as living sacrifices, holy and pleasing to God—this is your spiritual act of worship. Do not conform any longer to the pattern of this world, but be transformed by the renewing of your mind. Then you will be able to test and approve what God's will is—his good, pleasing and perfect will. (Romans 12: 1-2)

Imagination is not only the uniquely human capacity to envision that which is not, and therefore the fount of all invention and innovation. In its arguably most transformative and revelatory capacity, it is the power that enables us to empathize with humans whose experiences we have never shared.[13]

---

[13] Rowling, J.K. in a speech to the Harvard graduating class, 2011.

WHAT CAN A MISSIONAL IMAGINATION MEAN IN A LIFE?
Below is part of a letter that a friend of ours, a teacher, wrote to God about an experience where he was called to a missional imagination.

Dear God,
I know, God, that You were there in this experience, but it wasn't until now that I truly understand how having a missional imagination opened my eyes to You.

A few months ago, I had a student in my class that appeared to be very troubled. Well over age, stricken with poverty and life struggles that I wouldn't begin to understand or be able to relate to. This student walked to school every day rain or shine. It just happens that I would drive along his route and provide a ride for the last stretch. I never asked for a thank you and honestly never expected to get one; I just knew that as, a teacher, a coach, a good person that's what I should do. It never occurred to me that I should be picking this child up in the name of God—or that it might be You that I was picking up.

Weeks went by and I would occasionally pick this student up depending on whether or not I saw him. Until a few weeks ago. One day in class I reprimanded this same student for disrupting the class. Immediately he reacted by yelling too many obscenities to list and calling me everything under the sun. I was furious inside, knowing that I give this child a ride routinely without as much as a thank you and now this. I was so mad God, I didn't stop to think why this happened, I didn't stop to think at all. I just stuffed it away and went on with the day.

Well, a few days passed and I had stopped thinking about what had happened, until I turned that familiar corner and saw this student walking down the road. What am I supposed to do?, I thought. Honestly, I wanted to drive by and at first I did. I made it about 500 feet past him before putting the brakes on and pulling over. I just sat there, still furious at him. After a second, he got up to the truck, opened the door and climbed in. . . No hello, no good morning, not even a glance. For the next three minutes of the drive neither of us spoke to each other. I was still furious and didn't know what to say. He just sat another day of his life, I'm sure oblivious to me even being mad. As we got to the school, he opened the door and said, for the first time, "Thanks Mr. Richardson."

In this moment I know You were calling, God. In this moment I know it was You that I was seeing. Why had I not seen it before? God, You give me moments like these all of the time and I don't want to waste them by freezing up and not saying anything. Please help me to see You in my midst.

What can a missional imagination mean in a life? Can it transform our interaction with culture? First, let's examine the role of culture in our lives.

THE AMERICAN CULTURAL LANDSCAPE

Does culture shape us? Do our surroundings shape our identity? Bob Pittman, a former MTV chairman, once said, "At MTV we don't shoot for the 14-year olds, we own them."[14] Does culture own us? Do we see our lives

---

[14] Bob Pitman MTV Chairman *Dancing in the Dark: Youth, Popular Culture and the Electronic Media*

as being "owned," shaped, or guided by any forces outside of ourselves? As we have discussed previously, in order to find life, we must understand and name "the water in which we swim." Part of that water is the American context in which we live.

Why is context so important? In the passage from Romans, Paul urges us not to conform, but to be transformed by the renewing of our minds. Paul reminds us that, if we are to live out our faith, we must first see the world differently. The gospel is an alternative story about a missionary God, and it helps us view the world through another lens. It is the story of a God who can transform us and a God who is in the process of transforming this world. The truth is that this story competes with what our culture tells us. As William Willmon writes, "Sunday is the struggle over the question, 'who tells the story of what is going on in the world?'"[15]

Modern theologians, Darrell Guder, Michael Frost, and Anthony Robinson write about basic trends which shape the American cultural landscape.[16] Their findings can be summarized into four categories: modern self as consumer; community and isolation; search for meaning in a fragmented life; and the end of Christendom. We assert that these perspectives on American life shape our lives and, therefore, directly impact our calling and our lives as Christians. We have identified a question that, we believe, defines the heart of each trend. Do any of these questions resonate in your own life?

---

[15] Willimon, William H. Pastor: *The Theology and Practice of Ordained Ministry*. Nashville, TN: Abingdon, 2002. Print.

[16] Robinson, Anthony B. *Transforming Congregational Culture*. Grand Rapids, MI: W.B. Eerdmans Pub. 2003. Print.
Guder, Darrell L., and Lois Barrett. *Missional Church a Vision for the Sending of the Church in North America*. Grand Rapids, MI: W.B. Eerdmans Pub., 1998. Print.
Frost, Michael. *Exiles: Living Missionally in a Post-Christian Culture*. Peabody, MA: Hendrickson, 2006. Print.

WHAT MATTERS TO ME?
WHO IS WITH ME?
WHO AM I?
HOW DO I PROCLAIM MY FAITH?

WHAT MATTERS TO ME?

> Typical features of the Modern Self as Consumer:
> • An economy shaped and driven by technology and its advances;
> • All of life turned into commodity;
> • Endless choices;
> • A movement toward global economy and an expanding pervasive consumerism.

In 2008, David Brooks wrote that our consumer appetites have been at an all-time high. He says,

> "The deterioration of financial mores has meant two things. First, it's meant an explosion of debt that inhibits social mobility and ruins lives. Between 1989 and 2001, credit-card debt nearly tripled, soaring from $238 billion to $692 billion. By last year, it was up to $937 billion, the report said. Second, the transformation has led to a stark financial polarization."[17]

[17] Brooks, David. "The Great Seduction." *The New York Times - Breaking News, World News & Multimedia*. 10 June 2008. Web. 26 Aug. 2010.
<http://www.nytimes.com/2008/06/10/opinion/10brooks.html>.

Obviously, with the sub-prime crisis and the recession there has been a complete recalibration of the American economy. This crisis has caused many of us to ask questions about money and consumption. What place does money have in your life? Is being a consumer an essential part of the American identity?

Theologian Darrell Guder writes that the consumer confronts endless options. While this freedom may be enticing and promise power in many ways, its promises for the long term are empty, and it may leave the modern self disempowered. He writes, "The modern self as consumer is both pawn and player in this economic game: pawn because each person is the object of the push to consume, and player because each person depends on the jobs of the marketplace that drive the culture of consumption."[18] In many ways, we are part of an endless cycle of consumption where we often wonder how much is enough and where we might be willing to risk everything to have more. Is this the life to which God calls us?

WHO IS WITH ME?

Typical features of the Changing Face of Community and the Problem of Isolation:
• Radical forms of individuality producing isolation and aloneness;
• Loss of shared experience (community);
• Transient lifestyle;
• Multiple tasks and responsibilities that fragment time and space;

[18] Guder, Darrell L., and Lois Barrett. *Missional Church a Vision for the Sending of the Church in North America.* Grand Rapids, MI: W.B. Eerdmans Pub., 1998. Print.

A 2005 New York Times article described an increasing transient lifestyle which is more and more common in the United States.[19]

"Relo children do not know a hometown; their parents do not know where their funerals will be. There is little in the way of small-town ties or big-city amenities—grandparents and cousins, long-time neighbors, vibrant boulevards, homegrown shops—that let roots sink in deep. . . It's as if they're being molded by their companies," said Tina Davis, a top Alpharetta relocation agent for the Coldwell Banker real estate firm. "Most of the people will tell you how long they'll be here. It's usually two to four years."

The article profiles the life of Kathy Link as representative of this transient lifestyle. "Ms. Link and her husband, Jim, 42, a financial services sales manager for the Wachovia Corporation of Charlotte, N.C., belong to a growing segment of the upper middle class, executive gypsies." She is a veteran "relo", having moved three times in the past 10 years to help keep her husband's career on track. During any typical day, she will spend her time juggling the school and extra-curricular needs of her three daughters while her husband is out of town two to five days a week. What weighs on her is the daily grind and she admits she is beginning to feel the strain of her vagabond life. She says,

"It's like I'm on a hamster wheel. . . We haven't found a church. We went church shopping. I would find places my children liked and I didn't or that I liked and they didn't. We found one, but it's

---

[19] Kilborn, Peter T. "The Five Bedroom, Six-Figure Rootless Life." *The New York Times - Breaking News, World News & Multimedia*. 1 June 2005. Web. 26 Aug. 2010. <http://www.nytimes.com/2005/06/01/national/class/01ALPHARETTA-FINAL.html>.

a half-hour drive away. We don't have that kind of time." "It's all here," she said, "but it's an hour drive away. Here it's like, 'Get the heck out of my way.' It's like go, go, go. We're just going, going, going. I call it drowning. It's when you can't see the top of the water."

Why is Kathy drowning? Why is she feeling over-whelmed? What drives these emotions? Is it worth moving to other communities? Is this transient lifestyle healthy? The question for Christians is: what is driving the franticness of life? If it is motivated by self-interest and self-promotion, is it worth it? Is it the life to which God calls us?

WHO AM I?

> Typical features of the Search for
> Meaning & Identity:
> • Hunger for an over-arching story to give meaning and structure to life;
> • Job, career and identity defined by profes-sionalized roles and skills;
> • Pervasive influence of change;
> • Pluralism.

What is the first question someone asks you when you go to a party? Usually, it is your name followed by, "What do you do?" The integration of work and identity has never been closer. Darrell Guder writes, "When asked to identify themselves today, people commonly refer to their career, job title, employer or educational achievements. This response illustrates how the culture of modernity roots a person's identity in one's achievements and place in the social order, especially the economic order. What identifies people is their function—what they do rather than their character or their personal qualities."[20]

In our lives, there is a renewed hunger for purpose beyond work. More and more people are searching for a meaningful vocation with a larger significance. As Christians, what is our identity? Are we defined by what we do? Or are we defined by God's call and claim on our lives?

> *"Come, all you who are thirsty, come to the waters . . .Why spend money on what is not bread and your labor on what does not satisfy? Listen, listen to me and eat what is good and your soul will delight in the richest of fare." (Isaiah 55:1-2, NIV)*

HOW DO I PROCLAIM MY FAITH?

Some scholars and theologians, including Darrell Guder and Michael Frost, have argued that we live in a Post-Constantinian culture. Here, it is helpful to define terms. Guder describes Constantinianism as:

The legal establishment of the Christian church by the Emperor Constantine in the fourth century. This action made Christianity an official religion in the Roman Empire. Christendom refers to the resulting impact of the Christian church on the empire's dominant culture. Taken together, these actions meant that the church held both a legally established position that privileged its existence, and a moral influence in shaping the society that

---

[20] Guder, Darrell L., and Lois Barrett. *Missional Church a Vision for the Sending of the Church in North America.* Grand Rapids, MI: W.B. Eerdmans Pub., 1998. Print.

privileged its life and work.[21]

Guder and Frost argue that the historical period of Christianity being the "official religion"—that is, the era of Christendom—is over. No longer does government reinforce the importance of the church's role and no longer is there a cultural expectation for individual or corporate Christian participation. In our post-Constantinian culture, the church's status as the center of a community has faded and people have moved away from a cultural obligation to attend church. If these trends are true, how do they shape us? How are we to respond? Are we to retreat from culture?

A THIRD WAY: THE ART OF TRANSLATION

While God may call some to a monastic life of solitude, most of us do not sense this is our call. Most of us live very much in the world and often struggle to find our place in it as God's called people. Perhaps it would help if we recognize that an essential challenge in the gospel and culture debate is the art of translation. How can we translate the good news and its promise of abundant life here and now in this broken world? Darrell Guder writes,

> The gospel is always conveyed through the medium of culture. It becomes good news to lost and broken humanity as it is incarnated in the world through God's sent people, the church. To be faithful to its calling the church must be contextual, that is, it must be culturally relevant within a specific setting. . . Since everyone lives in culture, the church's careful study of its context will help the church to translate the truth of the gospel as goodness for the society to which it is sent.

---

[21] Guder, Darrell L., and Lois Barrett. *Missional Church a Vision for the Sending of the Church in North America*. Grand Rapids, MI: W.B. Eerdmans Pub., 1998. Print. As well as Frost, Michael. *Exiles: Living Missionally in a Post-Christian Culture*. Peabody, MA: Hendrickson, 2006. Print.

Moreover, because culture is not neutral, this discipline will assist the church to discern how it might be compromising gospel truth as it lives out its obedience to Christ the Lord.[22]

As we respond to our call as Christians to see differently, to, as Paul writes in Romans 12, be transformed by the renewing of our minds, one first step is to recognize that culture is not benign. Rather, it shapes us in complex ways—some healthy and wonderful as well as some which are not congruent with the gospel.

For too long the debate has been framed such that we have two options related to cultural pressures: (1) retreat from this "evil" or (2) turn a blind eye. What if the missional response is to transform culture? Perhaps, through the Holy Spirit, we are given the creative resources to find and live a third way. The missional life is the recognition that we are called and empowered to see (imagination) and respond (improvisation) to the larger reality of a missional God. What if what Paul meant by being transformed is to see and live as a part of a larger reality?

A CONVERSION OF THE IMAGINATION:
THE PRACTICE OF SEEING OUR WHOLE REALITY

What do you think of when you think of imagination? Do you think of "pie in the sky" daydreaming? As adults, many of us would say that having imagination is just not practical. It does not get things done. But what if imagination is essential for the missional life? Eugene Peterson says it this way,

We who are made in the 'image' of God have, as a consequence, imagination. Imagination is the

---

[22] Guder, Darrell L., and Lois Barrett. *Missional Church a Vision for the Sending of the Church in North America*. Grand Rapids, MI: W.B. Eerdmans Pub., 1998. Print.

capacity to make connections between the visible and the invisible, between heaven and earth, between present and past, between present and future. For Christians, whose largest investment is in the invisible, the imagination is indispensable, for it is only by means of the imagination that we can see reality whole, in context. What imagination does with reality is the reality we live by. . . When I look at a tree, most of what I "see" I do not see at all. I see a root system beneath the surface, sending tendrils through the soil, sucking up nutrients of the loam. I see light pouring energy into the protoplast-packed leaves. I see the fruit that will appear in a few months. . . I see all that, I really do—I am not making it up. But I could not photograph it. I see it by means of imagination. If my imagination is stunted or inactive, I will only see what I can use, or something that gets in my way.[23]

Recently, I (John) visited a group of Honduran pastors. These pastors had very little in terms of formal education or economic benefit. What was so amazing about them was their ability to weave scripture with their own personal stories. They were able to see their world (a very poor world at that) and God's work in it. These men and women, who did not have the luxury of any real or advanced academic education, could see the world through the lens of scripture much more clearly than their American counterparts. For me, that is a missional imagination. If faith is a way of seeing the world, the question for all of us is, "Can we see God at work in the world and in our own lives?" I wonder if we are open to that faith, or, has our culture shaped our vision in such a way that we are unable to see?

---

[23] Peterson, Eugene H. *Under the Unpredictable Plant: an Exploration in Vocational Holiness*. Grand Rapids, MI: W.B. Eerdmans, 1994. Print. (Emphasis added.)

As Christians we are called to a missional imagination which allows us to see our whole context and our whole reality. In a commentary on First Corinthians, Richard Hays writes,

> In order to form a Christian community identity within a pluralistic pagan world, [Paul] repeatedly calls his readers to a conversion of the imagination.[24]

Paul invites the Corinthians (and us) to see the world in dramatically new ways, in light of the values shaped by a missional God. Many of the problems at Corinth were caused by the Corinthians' understandable tendency to think and act in ways that were entirely normal within the cultural world of the Greco-Roman city. Is this not our problem as well? Are we thinking and acting in ways that respond primarily to our cultural context? Is God calling us to a conversion of the imagination?

WHY IMAGINATION: A CREATIVE RESPONSE
Recall the vignette that opened this chapter. In that moment, on an ordinary road, with a student, our friend was called to see differently and to respond. In the messy and honest moments of life, are we called to have a missional imagination? Are we called to see each other differently? Are we called to name the forces which shape us in order to better respond? Are these our challenges?

continue the conversation

1. Has our culture changed? Is it helpful to consider the critiques of the modern self as consumer, the transient nature of life, the issue of community, and the end of

---

[24] Hays, Richard B. *First Corinthians*. Louisville, KY: John Knox, 1997. Print.

Christendom? From your perspective, are they true? If so, which ones? If not, which ones?

2. Do you think that the cultural assumptions for attending church have changed? If so, how have they changed and what kind of effect do you think this will have on church?

3. A church member once said, "If we are faithful Christians, we will be out of step with the culture." Do you agree with that statement? What do you think that means? How are disciples of Jesus to exist in the world, remain true to God, and not isolate themselves from living out the gospel in the surrounding culture?

4. Is having a missional imagination important to living and seeing God at work in the world? Does it help us see our whole reality?

ideas for the road:
prayer of st francis of assisi

St Francis was one of the great Christian leaders who saw and lived differently. Try and make his prayer your prayer and see what happens.

> Prayer of St. Francis:
> Lord, make me an instrument of your peace;
> where there is hatred, let me sow love;
> where there is injury, pardon;
> where there is doubt, faith;
> where there is despair, hope;
> where there is darkness, light;
> where there is sadness, joy.
> Grant that I may not so much seek to be con-
> soled as to console;
> to be understood as to understand;
> to be loved as to love.
> For it is in giving that we receive, it is in par-
> doning that we are pardoned. It is in dying
> that we are born to eternal life. Amen.

playlist

"Give Me Your Eyes", <u>What If We</u> by Brandon Heath

chapter 5:
listening to the still
small voice

Our greatest fear should not be of failure but of suc-ceeding at things in life that don't really matter.[25]

THE GOD WHO CALLS & THE SCANDAL OF PARTICULARITY

In his biography entitled Tender Bar, J.R. Moehringer writes, "Slumbering in every human being lies an infinity of possibilities, which one must not arouse in vain. For it is terrible when the whole man resonates with echoes and echoes, none becoming a real voice." [26] Moehringer chronicles his boyhood search for identity, given the difficult context of his life in which his father, nicknamed The Voice, abandoned the family. Our stories may differ but, like Moehringer, many of us are searching, listening for the call from a voice which will give meaning to our lives. With the many voices seeking our attention, how do we discern God's true voice so we are not left with just echoes?

---

[25] Chan, Francis, and Danae Yankoski. *Crazy Love: Overwhelmed by a Relentless God*. Colorado Springs, CO: David C. Cook, 2008. Print.

[26] *The Tender Bar, a Memoir by J.R. Moehringer*. Web. 25 Aug. 2010. <http://www.tenderbar.com/>.

One of the premises affirmed in scripture is that God calls. Theologian Frederick Buechner writes,

> Vocation comes from the Latin vocare, 'to call', and means the work a person is called to by God. There are many kinds of voices calling you to all different kinds of work, and the problem is to find out which is the voice of God rather than of Society, say, or the Superego, or Self-interest...The place God calls you to is the place where your deep gladness and the world's deep hunger meet. [27]

Buechner's quote affirms that it is often hard to hear God's call because there are so many voices competing for our identity and soul. As our previous chapter noted these voices can be seductive and very compelling. So how do we hear God's call? Is it through a loud bang, a whisper or another person? To understand this, let's look at the scriptural narrative.

In the book, <u>Bible and Mission</u>, Richard Baukham writes that there is a pattern in the Bible illustrating how God works in the world by moving from the specific to the universal.[28] Over and over, God takes that which is small and particular and uses it to bless the entire world. Baukham cites the Old Testament call stories where individuals such as Abraham and David, as well as a country like Israel, are called to be a universal blessing to the world. Lesslie Newbigin calls this pattern the "scandal of particularity." He writes, "Humans expected that God would reveal God's self through a dominating presence but rather the scandal is that God came in the form of a

---

[27] Buechner, Frederick. *Wishful Thinking; a Theological ABC*. New York: Harper & Row, 1973. Print.

[28] Bauckham, Richard. *Bible and Mission: Christian Witness in a Postmodern World*. Grand Rapids, MI: Baker Academic, 2003. Print.

servant who was crucified."[29] It is scandalous that God would come in the form of a humble servant. God continued this scandal by choosing a small group of first-century Jews, and then us, to proclaim the good news to the ends of the earth. If this is true, can God call you and me?

WHAT IS CALL?

This word call requires some reflection. Consider your first impression of the word's meaning. Do you think of call as a singular event of a particular time to a specific service? Or, in God's commission, could it be that there are embedded many "calls to action"? What if being called means to use the individual gifts given by God in order to be a blessing in the world? That is, to be a witness to Christ's resurrection by being an instrument of God's love, is to live so that others may know and understand God in our midst (John 10:38). Then the question becomes how to answer this call in our daily lives. How are we to take our gifts and our longings and meet the world's great need?

It must also be said that we may be called in many different ways, and often through relationship with other people, as is evident in the biblical stories, and that we are called throughout our lifetime. In this way, we see that call is blind to the barriers of race, gender, age, profession. All God's people are included in God's call.

THE PLACE OF RESPONSE

In call, there is implicit response. It is something we hear (contemplate, pray, reason, feel) as well as something we do (action). Consider one's call as a middle place for hearing and doing to have shared occupancy. In the work of hearing, we uncover a place of being which

---

[29] Newbigin, Lesslie. *The Open Secret: Sketches for a Missionary Theology*. Grand Rapids: Eerdmans, 1978. Print.

makes room for receiving the Creator's ever-present invitation to relationship. In this place, we find the necessary energy to follow the call.

TYRANNY OF THE URGENT

One of the biggest challenges for us in discerning God's call is the "tyranny of the urgent".[30] Most people prefer to lead meaningful lives. They would like to serve but service is one option among many in a culture where, as sociologist Robert Wuthnow puts it, we "want it all." He writes,

> One of the clearest implications of these trends is what I have termed in some of my writing as "wanting it all." Americans want it all: jobs (two jobs in the case of couples) that support a comfortable middle-class suburban lifestyle involving a house not only with a white picket fence but also with a three-car garage; jobs that are also personally fulfilling, meaningful, and relatively free of stress; a warm community of friends in a neighborhood or church with whom to share dinner parties and go bowling; lovely, well-mannered children who, as Garrison Keillor says of the children in Lake Wobegon, are "all above average"; and lots of free time in which to pursue their hobbies and serve the needy...We are the products of what social scientists sometimes call a "revolution of rising expectations. We want it all.[31].

What if living a missional life means not wanting it all or doing it all? What if the abundant life Christ offers –"*I have come that they may have life and*

---

[30] Covey, Stephen R. *The Seven Habits of Highly Effective People: Restoring the Character Ethic*. New York: Fireside Book, 1990. Print.

[31] Schwehn, Mark R., and Dorothy C. Bass. *Leading Lives That Matter: What We Should Do and Who We Should Be*. Grand Rapids, MI: W.B. Eerdmans Pub., 2006. Print.

have it to the full" (John 10:10, NIV)—is not about "more" as in accomplishing more but is about making space for meaning? Maybe we sense a void in our lives but we can't define it, or find it. No matter what we do or try, we can't fill up the God-shaped space in our lives with any thing or person other than God. What if the longing we feel is not for a better job or a better relationship or more free time but is for Yahweh, Creator God? What then?

THE GENTLE WHISPER
In discussing call with many people, the conversation is often shaped by the wrong idea that only ordained folk are called. But scripture is clear that God calls ordinary people like you and me. Sometimes we respond in fear but God reassures us, "Do not be afraid for I am with you." Often, people feel God's call through a whisper. The following passage describing the call of Elijah is helpful:

> *"Then he was told, "Go, stand on the mountain at attention before God. God will pass by." A hurricane wind ripped through the mountains and shattered the rocks before God, but God wasn't to be found in the wind; after the wind an earthquake, but God wasn't in the earthquake; and after the earthquake fire, but God wasn't in the fire; and after the fire a gentle and quiet whisper. When Elijah heard the quiet voice, he muffled his face with his great cloak, went to the mouth of the cave, and stood there. A quiet voice asked, "So Elijah, now tell me, what are you doing here?" (1 Kings 19:11-13, The Message, emphasis added)*

What are you doing here? Why were you made? What if we hear God's call not through the earthquakes of life but through a daily whisper? There maybe be a quiet voice present deep in our soul which calls us to trust more, see more, and be more. If that is true, what is that voice saying to you?

continue the conversation

1. Do you think you can be called by God? Have you ever heard that still small voice? If so, what is it saying? If not, is there anything blocking you from hearing that voice?

2. Do you see the pattern in scripture of God taking what is small and ordinary and using it for a universal blessing? Do you think that could happen with your life?

3. Are you living your life as an emergency, constantly rushing from one activity to the next? If so, do you think this is the life God intends for you?

ideas for the road: who's calling?

This 2-part activity asks you to reflect on call stories from Scripture and on your own story.

Part I: Biblical Texts on Calling
In the following Biblical call stories, look for common themes and the ways of individual response:
• Genesis 12:1-5a
• Exodus 3:1-15, 4:10-17
• Judges 4:4-10
• 1 Samuel 16:1-13
• Isaiah 6:1-8
• Jeremiah 1:4-10, 20:7-9
• Luke 1:26-56
• Matthew 4:18-22
• John 3:1-16

• Acts 8:26-38 & 9:1-20

Part II: Composing a Life Story

Quakers have a saying, "Let your life speak." If your life could speak, what would it say? What are your gifts? Do you live under the tyranny of the urgent? Do you want it all? If so, do you think that impedes your ability to discern God's call in your life? What is the noise that drowns out the voice of God's still small voice? What is the call of meaning in your life?

What is your story?

Consider your life in light of a spiritual journey; that is, the intersection of your spiritual life with external events. You may wish to graph this relationship or make a list of high and low points in your life and the events surrounding them. Have you had moments of feeling very close to God? Have you had feelings of being far away from God? What was happening during those times in your life?

What are your gifts?

List three gifts that you think you have. (Examples: I love to play music, I love to write, I have some discretionary time, I love to teach.)

Putting it together

If we agree with Buechner that an individual's calling is the place "your deep gladness and the world's deep hunger meet," can you articulate what your call may be? What if there is a call in your life. Could you write it down? Write one sentence which describes how you might be able to use the gifts that God has already given to you towards God's glory.

playlist

"The Call", <u>The Best of Anointed</u> by Anointed

improvisation

living a missional life is an
invitation to respond creatively to
God's call and to understand the
transformative nature of
relationship.

But the hardest thing for me has been to play jazz. Because in jazz, I have had to put myself in my own context. Whereas, in classical music, everything is set up for you. You just have to learn how to play. In jazz, it's been very difficult, because I have had to create a context to learn how to play in, from an intellectual standpoint, from a philosophical standpoint, and from an actual standpoint in terms of recruiting musicians. That's been the most difficult thing.[32]

[32] "Wynton Marsalis Interview -- Page 4 / 8 -- Academy of Achievement." *Academy of Achievement*. Web. 26 Aug. 2010.
<http://www.achievement.org/autodoc/page/mar0int-4.>.

chapter 6:
the courage to improvise

A church which pitches its tents without constantly looking out for new horizons, which does not continually strike camp, is being untrue to its calling···we must play down our longing for certainty, accept what is risky, and live by improvisation and experiment. Hans Kung[33]

Be strong and of good courage, do not fear nor be afraid of them; for the LORD your God, He is the One who goes with you. He will not leave you nor forsake you. (Deuteronomy 31:6)

IS THE CHRISTIAN LIFE A SCRIPT OR STORY?

We must recognize that our lives are a part of a larger story and that is God's story. Our life does not follow a dusty script and the Bible is not a self-help book with ten steps towards a better life. We acknowledge the messy and unplotted nature of life. We know from our own experiences that all plans and decisions do not birth easily. But instead of fearing uncertainty, we can recognize that

---

[33] Hirsch, Alan. *The Forgotten Ways: Reactivating the Missional Church*. Grand Rapids, MI: Brazos, 2006. Print.

this freedom is a gift of God's love. God loves in freedom. We are not like chess pieces moved in the game of life. Our hope in faith is that no matter our circumstances, God is present and offers new life. Our hope amidst the messiness of life is the larger story of God's love towards God's people. This story begins with God creating out of nothing:

In the beginning God created the heavens and the earth. Now the earth was formless and empty, darkness was over the surface of the deep, and the Spirit of God was hovering over the waters. Genesis 1:1-2

THE HOLY SPIRIT: A CREATIVE GOD

What if we believe in a God who creates and who continues to create? In the first chapter of the book of Genesis, we read that God created the heavens and the earth from emptiness. Using the same Hebrew word employed by New Testament writers to describe the Holy Spirit in Genesis, "God breathed." The creative breath of God is life-giving to all creatures. What if this same spirit empowers us to create in the midst of our own lives, when we feel formless and empty, when we feel covered by darkness, when we find ourselves facing complex choices?

The story continues throughout scripture where we are encouraged that the Spirit is alive and with us. Isaiah 42:1 says, *"Here is my servant, whom I uphold, my chosen, in whom my soul delights; I have put my spirit upon him; he will bring forth justice to the nations."* What if this is the same Spirit that can be upon us? The Spirit is given to us by Jesus Christ. In John 20:21, Jesus said, *"Peace be with you. As the Father has sent me, so I send you".* He breathed on them and said to them, *"Receive the Holy Spirit."* This is the Spirit of creativity and new life, evidence of God's ongoing creative action in the world as well as an open invitation to participate. To be a part of this creative Spirit, you have to put yourself into God's story. You have to put yourself into the music.

THE CALL TO IMPROVISE: PUTTING YOURSELF INTO THE MUSIC

What if God's call is to put yourself into the music as Marsalis describes above—that is, to put yourself into God's story? What if the way our life intersects with God's story is not a script? We are faced with tough decisions and tough problems, but our call is to improvise, as we are guided by God's story. If we have the courage to improvise, we can't just play the old sheet music anymore. We have to be creative. We have to put ourselves out there in our "context." We have to risk putting ourselves in the unknown. If we trust that God will use us, we can do this. This might mean stepping out in faith by crossing borders racially, ethnically, socially. This might mean trying something new while the Spirit calls us to improvise. The question for all of us and the church is:

do we have the courage and the trust in a missional God to step out in faith and improvise based upon our call?

When I (John) served the congregation of Second Presbyterian Church in Indianapolis, Indiana, I was the liturgist and preacher for a casual service. For the service there was a great jazz trio called the Jack Gilfoy Trio. While the whole group was great, what made them such a special gift was their piano player, Marvin Chandler. Marvin was an elderly African-American preacher who could pray and preach. Marvin loved jazz and one day I asked him about jazz. He responded,

"I believe that, as an art form, jazz music's unique

contribution to art is that of improvisation – the almost spontaneous exercise of imagination and training—in producing an experience shared by the artist and the hearers. The improvisational stance is one of a moment full of possibilities that are met and honored. This is Creation, whose source and power is God!"

Samuel Wells, in his book *Improvisation*, writes,

Improvisation in the theater is a practice through which actors seek to develop trust in themselves and one another in order that they may conduct unscripted dramas without fear." He goes on to say, "this is a study of how the church may become a community of trust in order that it may faithfully encounter the unknown of the future without fear.[34]

What both Chandler and Wells tell us about improvisation is that it is vital for the missional life. Our cultural context breeds fear. In fear, improvisation stalls. As individuals, we are afraid of following God's call for many reasons, perhaps because it could mean making less money, not "having it all," or being different. In fear, instead of trusting God, we depend on tradition or the cultural script. We trust what has been done before, the safe-bet, or what everyone else is doing.

If we are willing to trust that God is alive and at work in the world, then what?

---

[34] Wells, Samuel. *Improvisation: the Drama of Christian Ethics.* Grand Rapids, MI: Brazos, 2004. Print.

IMPROVISATION: THE PRACTICE OF RESPONDING FREELY AND CREATIVELY TO GOD'S CALL

We are called to live a life of improvisation, trusting that we are not alone and that our lives can be part of a larger story. Improvisation encourages us to be creative and turn outwards, instead of cloistering in fear and doing what is safe. Improvisation challenges us to tap into our imagination, to be unconstrained by the reality around us and to have our lives point to a higher calling. Improvisation means we trust in the resurrection. The test for Christians is whether we can live out our faith with trust.

Do we believe that Jesus is alive? Do we believe that Christ is risen? If we do, then all things are possible. As Christians, the resurrection reality shapes our lives dramatically and, in fact, is the power behind a missional life. It is the belief that what we see as "reality" here and now is not the end of the story. We believe in a missionary God who is reconciling this world at this moment and in whom all things are possible. Are we willing to trust this reality?

LOVE MADE ME AN INVENTOR

L. Gregory Jones, dean of Duke Divinity School, tells the story about Marguerite "Maggy" Barankitse, a survivor of the civil war in Burundi between the Hutu and Tutsi factions. This extraordinary woman of faith experienced trial and tragedy in her life and in the life of her community yet did not give up hope. In fact, she declared that through the difficulties, "love made me an inventor." True to her own vision of God's call, Maggy has been a guiding force in the re-imagining of her village into a community she named Maison Shalom, which means "House of Peace."

Maggy's story goes back 15 years to the civil war in Burundi. When the Hutu militia came to her Tutsi community and massacred most of Maggy's extended family and many of her friends, she escaped with her seven adopted Hutu and Tutsi children and found refuge with Hutus in the compound of the Catholic bishop. But a group of Tutsis came to the compound to kill the Hutus there. Because she was a Tutsi, they spared Maggy, but as punishment for her adoption of Hutu children they stripped her, tied her up and forced her to watch the massacre of 72 people. Eventually she found her seven adopted children hiding in the church sacristy.

Maggy decided that she was going to rebuild her village as a place of peace. Even though she has never married, she adopted another 25 children, paying a significant price to the militia for their freedom. She now had more than 30 children, a desire to rebuild her village, and a heart full of love.

Maggy, a devout Catholic, believes that our identity as people created in the image of God is more fundamental than being a Hutu or a Tutsi. She is convinced that God's love is more powerful than hatred and violence.

Maggy built huts for children, developed a health clinic and a school, set up microfinance initiatives and instituted business training in hairdressing, auto mechanics and other vocations. She taught sustainable agriculture. She explained the power of God to foster reconciliation and create new life. She seemed intuitively to know how to embody the gospel in a community by developing the interconnections of a holistic understanding of salvation.

She also built a swimming pool and a film theater.

The swimming pool is on the site of tunnels that had served as a mass grave for casualties in the war. She says that she wants those waters to cleanse the children's imagination of the violence and immerse them in an alternative, joy-filled imagination. The allusions to baptism are clear and focused for Maggy. The film theater reminds the children that life is meant to be enjoyed, not merely endured, and that they are not simply victims of wars but human beings with dignity. Maggy even found funding for "Hollywood-style" theater seats. When rebel soldiers demanded payment in exchange for not destroying the theater, Maggy invited them to watch some movies instead (she taped a poster to the theater door indicating that weapons were not allowed). The rebels came to the movies.

Now the town also has a hospital and a nursing school—and a morgue. The morgue is important to Maggy because she believes that one teaches people how to live in part by taking care of those who have died.

Some of the first children to benefit from living in Maison Shalom have become teachers in the schools and community leaders. The huts are set up so the older children can become the caregivers for younger children. Over 30,000 children have benefited from Maison Shalom.

As my colleague was telling me about Maggy, the phrase force of nature kept coming into my mind for this amazing woman. Even patriarchal men in the area, who think women should stay at home and let the men lead, describe Maggy's leadership with awe and reverence.

Maison Shalom is an extraordinary resurrection story. The health clinic, hospital and nursing school have been built on the site of the village where Maggy's family was massacred. She narrates the story with a profound faith, a theological thickness and a Christian articulation that is stunningly beautiful. Love has made her an inventor, indeed. [35]

The story of Maggie encourages and inspires us to look at our lives. When circumstances confront us, how can we improvise? How can we believe, still, in a creative God who from the beginning of time has defined and challenged us into new life? What would it mean for our lives if we refocused? If we looked at one another with awe, as fellow persons loved by God? Perhaps it would change our lives and our relationships. Perhaps it would enlarge our hearts with room for all people. Perhaps it would stretch our minds and broaden our understanding of God. In so doing, perhaps it would lead to a redefining or the recreating of our world.

continue the conversation

1. Do you agree that the Bible is not a "10-step" self-help book but a living hope in the midst of the messiness of life? Why or why not? Do you see your life as part of God's story? Are you afraid to go "off-script" for God?

2. What does it mean to you to worship a creative God? What examples from your own life or from the larger

---

[35] Jones, Gregory L. "Maison Shalom."
Http://www.christiancentury.org/article/2009-06/maison-shalom. Christian Century, June-July 2009. Web.

world illustrate this aspect of God's nature?

3. Do you think improvisation is freeing as an idea? Is it a helpful framework for understanding the Christian, and the missional, life?

4. Are we called as Christians to be risk-takers? Can we trust God enough to take risks?

ideas for the road:
consider the text

Enlarge the place of your tent,
Stretch your tent curtains wide,
Do not hold back,
Lengthen your cords,
Strengthen your stakes.
Isaiah 54:2

playlist

"The Song is You", Marsalis Standard Time, Volume 1 by Wynton Marsalis

chapter 7:
a relational God and the importance of relationships

"If you want to go fast, go alone. If you want to go far, go with others." - African proverb

A LACK OF CONNECTION:

A few years ago my wife and I (John) chaperoned a group of senior high school students to Peru. We had accompanied similar groups for several years but this group was different. Two days into the trip, at 1:00 am, I was holding the head of an intoxicated high school student as he was vomiting after sneaking out. When he had finally eliminated everything from his stomach, he turned to me and said, "I want what you have. . . I want faith in something beyond myself."

Maybe this young adult was just drunk but the experience taught me an important lesson. These kids were from wealthy families and had everything they needed. They were academically competitive and probably had every opportunity to find success, yet something was missing. The culture had shaped them to be ultra-individualistic, and they had no sense that their actions might have consequences on the group. They had no sense of connection to each other except to get what they wanted.

As they walked around some of the poorer areas of Lima, I remember seeing how blind they were to the poverty and how it did not affect them as long as their desires were met. Our group fell apart and we had to send a number of kids home. In that moment, it was clear to me that the church has an essential calling to teach another way of living in community.

This small group was a microcosm of how ill-formed we can become. Our culture teaches us to see people and think, "what can this relationship do for me?" "What can I get out of this person?" Yet the gospel teaches us to see Christ in each other. The gospel calls us to live in community and to see our connection to each other as children of God. In such genuine relationship, we are invited to see others fully and to see beyond ourselves. We are called to love our neighbor as we love ourselves.

A LACK OF CONNECTION A RELATIONAL GOD IN THE TIME OF FACEBOOK FRIENDSHIPS

In the book, *Bowling Alone: The Collapse and Revival of American Community*, author Robert Putnam describes current U.S. society as becoming increasingly individualistic.[36] Using the example of trends in bowling, Putnam writes that, although the number of people who bowl has increased in the last 20 years, the number of people who bowl in leagues has decreased. He found that there is less and less social interaction, which he attributes to a lack of investment in community. However we, as Christians, believe that we are created *for* com-

[36] Putnam, Robert D. *Bowling Alone: The Collapse and Revival of American Community*. New York: Simon & Schuster, 2000. Print.

munity. What we understand from scripture is that we can't make it on our own. We are created for relationship. But is real relationship difficult to find?

Our world seems hyper-connected and yet is there a depth to the vast network of our relationships? Is Facebook redefining our sense of friendship? With a click of a button, we become "friends" but does true friendship and real community take more? To participate in true community, we might be inconvenienced. To sustain and develop relationships, we must decide to invest time and energy. Relationships involve freedom, trust, intention, presence,and patience. But who has time for all that? Yet deep down, all of us yearn for relationships and community. As we often read in biographical works of the rich and famous, a person's life may be full of "success" in the form of material possessions, an expansive lifestyle, numerous accolades, and powerful sway but as life nears its end, the person faces the realization that the price of success was at the expense of relationships. That what was essential was not the power but the people.

The challenge of community in contemporary society is explored in the film *Up in the Air*. It is the story of a successful executive, Ryan Bingham, whose treasure chest is filled with mileage and hotel award points but little in the way of meaningful relationships. He is isolated from family yet constantly surrounded by the faces of strangers. He is a modern road warrior –his life in the air is defined by freedom from relationships. "Moving is living," he quips, and he consistently seeks to avoid attracting permanent attachments. He recognizes that relationships are the "heaviest things in our lives" and, preferring to travel light, he strives to discourage them.

Ryan's story is not unique in America. Perhaps some of us have been convinced of the clarity of this dream of being able to do it on our own, and even when we find that we cannot, we hesitate to reach out. We know that relationships involve cost and risk and can feel burdensome at times. Yet at the core of our being, and through real encounters in our lives, we also know that we can experience the fullness and richness of life through the complexity of relationships. They can be a portal to understanding forgiveness and grace, to experiencing healing and humility, and to finding joy and humor. That in community we can learn about God's love for us.

CHURCH COMMUNITY

Committing to community is messy. It is not easy. We are different. It can be slow. Especially in a church! But what do we really believe about the role of the church community in our lives? Is church a service provider? Is the Spirit a commodity to be consumed? Is faith about instant gratification?

The model of Christian community portrayed in scripture is very different. It is, in fact, counter-cultural. As in the example of the early church chronicled in the book of Acts, the church does not exist for personal good but for a common good. In scripture, we learn that community means we must strive to live with others who are not like us. We are strong and weak, eyes and feet, Jew and Greek, Republican, Democrat, Libertarian, Green, CNN watchers, FOX TV lovers, young, old...and yet! All of us are invited into relationship with God. Despite our differences, we are all invited into an unfolding story of God's persistent love. A story where Father, Son, and Holy Spirit are sent in redeeming love to restore a broken creation.

UNITY IN OUR WEAKNESS

Often along the journey we find that what we have in common in community is not strength but weakness. The theologian Henri Nouwen writes, "We are unified by our common weaknesses, our common failures, our common disappointments and our common inconsistencies."[37] True community is united not in our strength but in our common weakness and our common need. We acknowledge our need for God and for each other. An important affirmation for us as Christians is to be honest about our limitations and to be open to admitting that we cannot make it alone. But in an individualistic world that can be a difficult affirmation.

GOD IN THREE PERSONS

Relationships are central to living a missional life because we believe in a relational God. When we consider the triune God –Creator, Redeemer, Sustainer—we can see that the essence of God is relationship. In the Trinity of Father, Son, and Spirit, we see perfectly modeled fellowship, where there is distinction between the three persons but unity in mission. The relationship itself is sentient to the life of God. God exists in relationship, so as Christians, we are called to a missional life through relationships.

In the gospel of Matthew, the Pharisees test Jesus with this question: *"Teacher, which is the greatest commandment in the Law?" And Jesus replies, Love the Lord your God with all your heart and with all your soul and with all your mind. This is the first and greatest commandment. And the second is like it: 'Love your neighbor as yourself.' All the Law and the Prophets hang on these two commandments." (Matthew 22:37-40)*

If we believe in Jesus' words, that we are to love our neighbor as ourselves, then we are created to be in relationship.

---

[37] Yaconelli, Mike. *Messy Spirituality*. Grand Rapids, MI: Zondervan, 2007. Print.

With this understanding of the Trinity and of Jesus' teaching, we make three important statements about believing in a relational God. First, we recognize that interconnectedness between persons begins in the Trinity, where three are one and where there exists mutuality and individuality. This is our model for community, partnership, and friendship. Secondly, we affirm that mission is not something we do "to another" but "with another." Our attitude toward each other is not "them" but "us." The model for this perspective is a God who does not force or coerce but who loves in freedom and empowers through the Holy Spirit. Third, it highlights our own need for intimacy with our neighbor. While we may be able to help others with basic needs (food, education, shelter, etc.), we also long to be known. We hunger for authentic relationships.

"Do you love me?"

> When they had finished eating, Jesus said to Simon Peter, "Simon son of John, do you truly love me more than these?" "Yes, Lord," he said, "you know that I love you." Jesus said, "Feed my lambs." Again Jesus said, "Simon son of John, do you truly love me?" He answered, "Yes, Lord, you know that I love you." Jesus said, "Take care of my sheep." The third time he said to him, "Simon son of John, do you love me?" Peter was hurt because Jesus asked him the third time, "Do you love me?" He said, "Lord, you know that I love you." Jesus said, "Feed my sheep." (John 21:15-17)

In this passage, Christ asks Peter, "Do you love me?" The ensuing conversation between Peter and Jesus teaches us many things. It is an act of grace and absolution offered to Peter who previously had denied Christ before the people. It is an instruction to take care of one another. It is a command to follow Christ. But in reading this story, we are struck by the very asking of the question for, as Peter confesses, surely divine Christ must have known the reality and depth of Peter's love. Yet, Jesus still asked. Perhaps in order to teach us about relationship, Jesus embodies an example of relationship, to love and be loved, to know and be known. In Jesus' response to Peter's affirmation, "Feed my sheep," Jesus reveals who he is, what he is about, and where his heart lies.

When Christ knocks at the door of our lives, perhaps he asks the same question of us, "Do you love me?" Yes, in order that we follow Christ and are reminded of God's grace and re-energized for the feeding of sheep but also so that we respond to Jesus' question regarding our relationship. In the obedience of following, we are primarily engaged in an act of love. Jesus is known and loved in our act of loving and serving one another. In our humble acceptance of God's love, we participate in relationship with God. Christ knows and loves us. Christ asks that we return the favor. For it is that our relationship with Creator, Redeemer, Sustainer God indeed "feeds" all other amity. Our love for others is in response to the love God lavishes upon us.

Grateful for God's love and mindful of the instruction to love our neighbor, we turn to the question:

who is my neighbor?

DOES IT MATTER TO ME?
One of the huge shifts in the recent world is our increasing interconnectedness. From global nuclear proliferation to terrorist acts on American soil, from economic crises in the third world to those on Wall Street, we are all connected. In the constant clamor of internet and media voices vying for our attention, the world is becoming more connected. When we learn of massive devastation on the other side of the world we want to act, yet

we feel overwhelmed by the suffering in the world. We feel stretched to reach out to the homeless man on our local streets even as we are bombarded with pleas for help from overseas. We become aware of the statistic that 40% of the world's population lives on less than $2 a day and we ask "what does this matter to me?" We learn that:

[indent statistics]- Americans make up 5% of the world's population but consume 50% of the world's resources.
- Over one billion kids do not have access to schools, one child in four has to work rather than go to school, and half of the world's children live in poverty.
- Over one billion people have unsafe drinking water, and 40% of the world lacks basic sanitation.
- The problem of hunger in the world is not the earth's inability to produce food for 6.5 billion people but the inequitable distribution of that food.

What are we called to do with these statistics? As we realize the interrelated nature of the world, the question "Who is my neighbor?" becomes increasingly significant. It can seem easy to do nothing when confronted by the enormity of the world's challenges and suffering, and in light of our own relative ease, but is this the approach that satisfies? What if, recognizing our own limitations as well as God's power, we look at the question through the lens of improvisation? Then we are open to seeing each other with new eyes and trusting that God will work through us. We recognize the need for community and that we are not called to do all things alone;rather, we respond through discernment when Christ calls.

HOW DO WE RESPOND TO OUR NEIGHBOR
In the following story, Ellen shares an encounter with poverty that many of us have faced in our daily lives.

What am I called to do, where do belief and action intersect, when I am minding my own business, and making good time to bring my children to my in-law's house, and there is a man at the base of the exit ramp on I-26E proclaiming himself to be homeless and hungry? He certainly looks the part. A bag at his feet, a worn cardboard sign in his chapped palms, bedraggled hair and clothes. Apples come to mind –the three in the cooler in my minivan—healthy, crisp, delicious. I roll down my window as I pull toward the stop sign and offer the apples to him. He takes them, seeming grateful, yet honestly points out that he lacks the teeth for biting into one. Not for me to worry, he explains, he'll get a plastic knife at a convenience store. I search my mind to recall if I have one in my vehicle but come up empty. I apologize to the man, who quickly absolves me, and I go on.

My boys and I have the briefest of a conversation about this exchange. The six year-old says, "Really? He doesn't have a home, at all?" Later, after depositing them with their grandparents, I stop at the gas station store and purchase a large bottled water and a box of plastic utensils. I have already remembered other packaged snacks in the car: multi-grain chips, granola bars. I put these in a paper bag, with the water, utensils, and some napkins. I drive back around to approach the exit ramp from my earlier direction. The man is gone. I drive back and forth a bit, scouting out the adjoining exit ramps, but never find him. I feel deflated by my meager witness. This encounter is far from figured-out or answered-up.

CATCH AND RELEASE FRIENDS

The book Same Kind of Different as tells the true story of an unlikely friendship between Ron and Deborah Hall, two rich white folks from suburban Fort Worth, and Denver Moore, a homeless African-American gentleman who had lived on the streets for years.37 Their friendship begins one day when Deborah encourages her reluctant husband Ron to go down to the homeless mission in Fort Worth. Ron describes the discomfort of going that day. It was way out of his comfort zone. In fact, he compares what he saw at the Mission in downtown Fort Worth to a scene from out of Mad Max.

On the way home, after that first day, Ron recalls that Deborah stopped him and said, "I had a dream. . . I saw the [homeless mission] changed. In my dream, it was beautiful, flowers and everything. She said to Ron, "Can't you just see it? No trash in the gutters. Just a beautiful place where people can know God loves them."

Through her dream, Deborah feels called to act. In those first few visits Ron writes that Deborah would serve everyone with respect and hospitality. He writes, "I am sure they [folks at the shelter] thought Deborah was on amphetamines, or possibly running for mayor, as they had likely never seen anyone who smiled and asked the questions as much as she did. She would say, 'Hi, I'm Deborah and this is my husband Ron.'" He goes on to say, "She was forever telling rough-looking characters with names like Butch and Killer, 'Oh what a pretty name!'"

One person in particular comes to Deborah's attention. She feels especially called to reach out to and become friends with a man named Denver Moore, who is a loner and feared in the Mission circles. Denver grew up on a cotton farm, the product of segregation, and he describes his own story which includes catching a freight train, scrapes with the law, Angola prison, and being homeless for a lot of years. But "Miss Debbie", according to Denver, was "pushy" and persistent enough to take an interest in Denver and they develop a friendship.

In a frank conversation Denver says to Ron, "Now many folks would come and serve once or twice and we never see them again. But you and your wife come every week. . . and your wife is always asking everyone his name and his birthday." (also commenting that everyone at the shelter thinks they are working for the CIA!) In a moment of honesty Denver asks Ron, "What do you want from me?" Ron replies, "I just want to be your friend." A week later in one of the most powerful moments of the book, Denver asks Ron if he is serious about his invitation to be a friend. The dialogue continues:

Denver says, 'There is something that that I heard about white folks and it bothers me, and it has to do with fishing. I heard y'all catch and release. That really bothers me. Ron, if you fishing for a friend you just going to catch and release, then I ain't got no desire to be your friend. But if you looking for a real friend, then I'll be one, forever.

That promise is kept and this unlikely friendship is solidified. In the final chapter Denver says, "I used to spend a lot of time worrying that I was different from other people. After that, I met Miss Debbie and Mr. Ron, I worried that I was so different from them that we would never going to have a future. But I found out everybody's different, the same kind of different as me. We're all just regular folks walking down the road God done set in front of us."

Part of living a missional life is recognizing our interconnectedness as the children of God. We must acknowledge that our lives have consequences to others, and that we are relational beings who long for intimacy and

friendship.   We seek friendships where we can laugh
and be known.   We need community where we can be
supported and loved as we journey down the road together.

WHERE ARE YOU IN THE STORY?
During a devotional gathering at the end of a trip to
Honduras, one of the people in the mission group shared
the story of the starfish.

[indent story] Someone walking along the beach notices
a person throwing starfish back into the sea.   There are
hundreds and thousands of starfish stranded on the
shore.   The situation seems to be a rather futile effort!
The onlooker approaches this individual and says, "Why
are you doing throwing starfish into the ocean? It won't
make a difference."   To which the person replies simply,
"It makes a difference to that one starfish."

Many in the group identified with the person in the story
who was doing the throwing.   And this story is helpful for
dealing with feelings of being overwhelmed when faced
with issues of poverty.   Then another person in the group
spoke up, "No, wait...what if we are the starfish?"   Indeed, what if we are the ones in need?   What if we are
the starfish in need of being thrown into the vastness of
God's love?"   What if Jesus is the thrower?

Perhaps true community comes when we put ourselves
in the story not as the thrower but as the starfish.   If the
key to living a missional life is a radical commitment to
relationship, community, and service to our neighbor,
then it means lifting up the common good even when it
is not convenient.   It means that from a place of honesty, we can experience God's love, together, as a community. In living a missional life, we begin when we acknowledge our need for God and for each other, naming
our deep desire for relationship.   We begin living in

community when we humbly ask God to fill our lives and help us invest in spiritual relationships. Even though it is messy, time-consuming, and risky, we remember that we can't make it alone. Are you willing to invest in relationships?

continue the conversation

1. Does considering the relational nature of God change or enlarge your ideas about "mission"? How would you describe your interconnectedness with God and with the world?

2. In your life, do you find it difficult to develop authentic friendships (to know and be known)? Do you agree that culture often preys on our need for true friendship without offering corroboration? Can you think of ways we deter ourselves from developing relationships based on trust?

3. Consider your life. Who is your neighbor? Does Jesus' instruction to us to love our neighbor, joined with the story of the Good Samaritan (Luke 10:25-37), challenge any assumptions you have about neighbor?

4. Did reading the story of friendship between the Halls and Denver Moore inspire you to listen for God's call to you? If so, how?

ideas for the road: crossing boundaries

Be encouraged to step out of your comfort zone into the stretching zone. Some ideas include (1) commit to meeting with a friend or acquaintance in your community to talk about how you have seen God at work in your life; (2) spend time in parts of your community which are unfamiliar or foreign to you and meet people who are not like you; (3) bless another person this week through your love, words, or deeds.

improvisation

playlist

"One", <u>African Spirit</u> by U2 with Soweto Gospel Choir

incarnation

living a missional life is to
trust in a living God.

The opposite of love is not hate but is indifference.
—Elie Wiesel

chapter 8:
stories of hope & people
who inspire

Part of living a missional life is responding to the call to reach out to, and be in relationship with, our neighbor. To faithfully enter into relationship where two can walk with another, dream with another, and work alongside one another. A missional life is the humble recognition that we need each other. A missional life considers that God, as an incarnational God, places people in our lives for a reason and then asks that we keep our eyes open for the opportunity of reaching out toward a relationship where two are united in Christ.

In this chapter, we share stories of people who are living missional lives. Pam, George, Debbie, and Kathy are very different people who have faced tremendous adversity. Yet, they looked beyond the current reality and responded to God's call in creative and inspiring ways. Often going on just faith or belief, they embody the principles of integrity, imagination, and improvisation. Our hope is that their stories will inspire you to look around and to listen for God's call in your life.

pam sloat and pattison's academy

CAN YOU TELL THE STORY OF PATTISON'S ACADEMY?
Pattison's Academy was founded to recognize and address that children with severe disabilities have a significant capacity to learn and a right to maximize their potential (whatever that may be).   In 2006, my husband Mark and I, along with three professional women we met as a result of our daughter PJ, founded the Pattison's organization. The mission is to improve the quality of life for children with multiple disabilities by providing comprehensive education and rehabilitation programs. We set out to create a school program to prevent children and families from falling through the cracks, to advocate for improving the child's quality of life through access to integrated health and education service models, to leverage the available resources in the community to create

a more sustainable and efficient infrastructure for all children with disabilities, and to reduce the risk of families who are caring for these children in the community from falling into poverty. We are trying to create an enablement model to prevent a cycle of disablement that affects the whole family for generations.

WHERE HAVE YOU SEEN GOD IN THIS JOURNEY?
Even before I was married. I worked for Blackbaud (a technology company in Charleston, SC) and though I liked what I did, I would sit at my desk and think there had to be more to life than the 8:30 a.m. to 5:00 p.m. grind. It paid well, but it just didn't fulfill me. I knew there was something more tugging at me but I wasn't sure what it was. I have always been someone who likes a challenge and sticks up for those who don't seem to be able to do it for themselves. I think God knew I needed an outlet for that. To me, it does not mean that God caused PJ's condition in order to test me. Rather, I think God knew that when PJ came along he could give me the strength to rise to the occasion. When PJ was born, once Mark and I got through the "fog," we started moving forward. I am not sure where the energy for this movement came from. Some might say it was denial or my way of dealing with depression, anger, or the myriad of overwhelming emotions. I just know for me, I needed to direct my fear, anger, confusion, energy, and need for mental stimulation toward something that would make a difference for PJ and others like her. This drive, coupled with an almost insane hunger to learn, investigate, get to the bottom of things and find out why things work the way they do so they can be better, started Mark and I on our path. Whenever we have reached a point with either PJ's health or Pattison's Academy where we didn't know what to do, God has provided a way. It isn't easy and it means lots of hard work, but when we haven't known what to do or it seemed like the end on many levels,

things would finally come together. I have so many examples of this, it is hard to narrow down:

We needed a place to have the first camp. I happened to run into our pastor at the park with his children while I had PJ and Amelia (Mariana wasn't even a thought yet) and He offered the church. There was some negotiating and I learned a lot, but it all worked out.

Mark lost his job with Benefit Focus not too long after PJ was diagnosed. Even though he hated his job and the long hours, and I was stressed at home dealing with PJ's medical needs, his job had paid the bills. We were scared to death and not sure what to do, but decided to take the girls to the circus (When things are crazy, sometimes you have to go with it; the circus seemed like a good fit at the time, especially since we had free tickets.) At the circus, we ran into a friend of ours who was working for a company that was looking for an employee with Mark's skills. The job included a pay raise and better hours, and ended up being what we needed at the time for our family.

When we found out I was pregnant with Mariana, we had no idea how we were going to handle a baby in the midst of starting Pattison's Academy. We were short on money and time but she has been such a blessing and there is not a day that goes by that I am not totally thankful for the gift of her. Because of what we went through trying to get PJ diagnosed and stable, Mark and I don't really remember Amelia as a toddler. PJ didn't meet those milestones so Mariana is giving us the gift of those years we feel we missed.

Last summer, after the charter application for the school was approved through Charleston County School District without a hearing (which is unprecedented); we were trying to find a location and were coming up with nothing!

We were scared to death that we would never find a place that would meet our needs. Because I knew we needed publicity, I agreed to an interview with The Post and Courier. Right after the article was printed, a pastor from Rutledge Baptist Church called and said we needed to see what he had because he knew we needed to be there. It was more than we could possibly imagine! It was not without work, but it came together.

While all of this was going on, Mark was unemployed for 19 months. He had been talking with a company for over a year about a job he really wanted. COBRA had run out and we just couldn't afford to pay for family health insurance. Savings were gone, credit cards maxed. Mark somehow managed to keep a roof over our heads with odd jobs, but we were tapped. We didn't know what we were going to do. It was bleak. Then the very next month, one day out of the blue, the company called Mark and hired him. You cannot tell me that there is not a divine hand in that. God's timing is always incredible.

I have always had this unexplainable feeling that something beyond anything that I can comprehend will help me do the right thing for the right reasons in the right way if I just listen to my gut. I am not a "people" person; I get nervous, and can seem cold and harsh. Knowing this, God has brought people into my life who are so different from me in that regard, including a few close friends whom I trust implicitly and who enable me to do what I do. Most importantly, one of those people is my husband Mark. We are two strange pieces of a complicated puzzle that just seem to fit. When I am spinning off into orbit completely stressed about something, he is the calm one who makes me laugh. When I am under a deadline and tend toward being a total workaholic, he is the one who makes me stop and give thanks for what I have around me. When I have been ready to just walk away from our marriage, he is the strong one who stays and holds us together until it gets better because too often just when we want to quit is exactly the time we are needed most. He has shown me that listening skills and patience can make all the difference. He has the weight of the world on his shoulders but most people would never know that. He is the smartest, strongest, most loving person I know, and God gave him to me to make me a stronger and better person. There is not a day that goes by that he doesn't drive me crazy, but I love him for it and I thank God for him.

FROM YOUR STORY WHAT ENCOURAGEMENT WOULD YOU GIVE TO OTHERS?

I think God put us on this earth to support each other and the things on it; to be the caregivers for each other. I believe our attitudes control so much of the impact we have on humanity; that living is about doing what will make you see things that are beyond yourself. Do something because it will help someone or something else, not because it is easy or because you think it will get you into heaven. Do it because it needs to be done. Surround yourself with people you can learn from, who compliment you, who mitigate or balance your own weaknesses. Talk to the people you don't agree with, listen to them, and respect their point of view. Then rise to it or above it to make a difference in the world around you. Show your own peace through your actions. God listens to me, and when I listen to God, things work out.

Please visit the Pattison's Academy website...
www.pattisonsacademy.org

george srour and building tomorrow

CAN YOU TELL THE STORY OF BUILDING TOMORROW?
I served as an intern with the World Food Program and had the opportunity to work both in Rome at the organization's world headquarters and then in Kampala, Uganda at one of their regional offices. While I was in Kampala, I studied the effectiveness of a school feeding program that was designed with the sole mission of improving school attendance. To do this, students and their families were promised food in exchange for coming to class. As I toured these sites, I began to realize the very poor conditions in which students were learning. One school was being held in an open room, perhaps 40x100 feet in dimension and it had over 500 kids crammed into the space. There were four classes being offered, one in each corner; clearly ineffective. The scene begged the question: what can I do to make an impact here?

When I returned to William & Mary for my senior year, I made it a goal to raise $10,000 for the construction of a new facility at that particular school. On Thanksgiving, I launched a campaign called Christmas in Kampala. A number of friends, administrators and people at the college who were instrumental in getting things started. In six weeks, we quadrupled our goal as we brought in $42,000! Our story appeared in newspapers far and wide and, on Christmas Day, we handed over a check, in Kampala, to the school for the construction of a brand new facility.

Building Tomorrow (BT) was born out of this experience and lots of careful thinking. We realized the big infrastructure needs were in the rural areas where many kids learn under trees or don't learn at all. Today, BT works with campus chapters at about 30 colleges nationwide to raise the funds necessary to pay for materials at each of our BT Academies. Local villages provide land and unskilled labor and the government of Uganda pays for the teachers. This week we're breaking ground on our 10th BT Academy. We serve about 1,500 kids today, and will double that number in the next 12 months.

WHERE HAVE YOU SEEN GOD IN THIS JOURNEY?
This is a trick question. Everywhere. There's really no explaining certain things that have happened without pointing to a divine influence on what we've been able to do. I find a great beauty on our college campuses seeing people of all faiths coming together. They are bound by a determination to make the world a better place by providing an education to children they've never met, and fueling this dream through the wackiest, craziest events you can imagine.

There have been several times when I've had to sit and ask myself, "What on earth am I doing and why am I here?" I've opened up my bank account to see $23 in it. I've been excited to open a new school only to find out that the bolts from all the trusses have been stolen for sale on the black market. I've sat in meetings where agreements we've had signed have been tossed aside. From the highs and the lows and especially everything in between, it's been reaffirming to know that God has kept His watch over our work and looks after BT in so many ways.

The truth is that I feel called to be where I am to-day—where my gifts and talents can hopefully be used to make an impact and live out what I believe.

FROM YOUR STORY WHAT ENCOURAGEMENT WOULD YOU GIVE OTHERS?

Have faith. There have been many points along the road when I've had no idea what will come next, how we'll solve a problem that has arisen, or how I'll be able to pay our staff. In fact there are many situations in which I find myself where I can honestly say I have no idea what I'm doing, especially when I'm meeting with our team in Uganda and trying to challenge the way we operate our model or how we construct a certain aspect of a building. I've had to realize on several occasions that none of the above will be solved on my own or even with others. The best thing I can do for myself and for the organization is to have faith and trust that we'll be able to navigate the next big hurdle, whatever that might be.

Please visit the Building Tomorrow website at... www.buildingtomorrow.org

friendship house: two voices

debbie sterken

CAN YOU TELL THE STORY OF THE FRIENDSHIP HOUSE?

The story of Friendship House is part of a journey, and remains a sentinel event in our son Rob's life as well as the life of our immediate family. The story starts soon after the shock of birth with a very sick baby who faced odds stacked against him in most every area. As the darkness lifted, we found our family surrounded by new friends who supported and accepted us. Rob's biggest advocates helped us transition into inclusive education, a regular kid on the block, and t-ball. In the early years, we faced frustration and hard work yet we sensed a wonderful appreciation for who Rob was and the strengths he brought to our family and everyone surrounding him.

Still, during those years, knowing that Rob would out-live us, the future looked very scary. Total independence for Rob would not be feasible so I started looking into group homes, both state and religious affiliated institutions in the area. It was a gut-wrenching process for me. I realized that Rob would not thrive in this situation, nor could I ever put him into a place that would not allow him some independence. There was no road map to follow. What should we do? I gave this question much time, worry, prayer and tears. Since his siblings were going off to college, as Rob graduated from high school, he thought he should be doing something similar. At this point, the coach of Hope College Basketball recruited Rob to be the manager, surpassing our wildest dreams! It gave Rob an opportunity for growth, independence and time with the "normal" population.

At this time, I heard that Western Seminary (in our town) was in the market for more student housing. My initial thought was that we could purchase a two-family house near the seminary. We would recruit a couple to live in one apartment and Rob and friend would live in the other apartment. This solution would give Rob some independence, socialization, and supervision. When the Dean of Students and I happened to walk out of church together, I seized the chance to share our idea of establishing a cooperative living situation. The Dean considered and supported the idea enough to pitch it to the administration and the board. Bob and I gathered some friends who might be interested in the concept and we met for several years around the dining room table to flesh out the project. We could not have built the Friendship House without an institution that would embrace this type of living situation.

WHERE HAVE YOU SEEN GOD IN THIS JOURNEY?
I see God in Rob. He radiates goodness, kindness and great humor about life. He gets the big picture and does not let the petty interrupt relationships with the people in his life. While he clearly understands when he is not kindly or fairly treated, he always gives that person

a second chance.   He wants the best for everyone and will work at making that happen.   Our family stories are often of Rob giving counsel to one of us, and damn if he isn't always pitch perfect!   Rob has forced all of our hands to have a godly perspective for all the people who must live on the fringe of society.

God has shown himself through so many relationships. Ironically, Marilyn, my atheist neighbor, and her son Michael have been the most Christ-like people in the life of our family.   Michael has been an angel and constant companion for Rob.   Through being a regular kid and watchful buddy, Michael set the tone in how one treats people with disabilities and unknowingly taught the high school kids how to treat kids like Rob more than any educator could do.

My husband Bob is the constant from day one.   When the world turned so dark, he encouraged me that we would make our family one full of love and joy.   Our kids also show me that God is present.   I continue to be amazed at their view of the world and people.

FROM YOUR STORY WHAT WOULD YOU SHARE WITH OTHERS?

I have learned that I often prefer to be with those who live and dance on the outside edge of life, for they are honest and thoughtful and unable to get hung up on the petty things.   What a shame it would be not to have learned that lesson! So one piece of advice I would offer is to live and love those who are weaker, for they have a story to tell and it is usually more God-like.   I have also learned that one has to do the hard work and can't rely on institutions to provide leadership -it is a grassroots kind of thing.   I believe that to advocate for the powerless is a role of the church.   I am heartened to be asked to share our story and hope it encourages more people to be interested in being an advocate.

kathy vanderBroek

CAN YOU TELL THE STORY OF THE FRIENDSHIP HOUSE?
Our story began when our son Seth was born with Down Syndrome and we were faced with the challenge of building a welcoming world for his future. With a child whose entire life will be shaped by "defects" of birth, all decisions quickly take on an entirely new perspective to become, not matters of choice, but matters of asking others to stretch themselves to learn how to embrace someone who is a little bit out of their ordinary. Seth and Rob were born almost 30 years ago, which has meant that almost every step in their lives has brought them to new crossroads and "trail-blazing" opportunities. Every step required us, as parents, to gently shepherd others to be brave and take a risk. For us, Friendship House is one of many dreams for all families like us, who want the world to be kind and friendly to their children, whoever they are.

While impressive in scope and beauty, Friendship House is not a culminating point for Seth and Rob. It is a stopping place, perhaps for 10 years, to hopefully provide families respite in order to problem-solve for the next leg of the journey. Where that leg will take us, what it will look like and who will be partners, is all up in the air. Life with an individual with special needs forces one to be able to live on the edge, like it or not. Life with an individual with special needs, no matter what that need might be, is a journey toward solutions, one after another after another. It doesn't stop.

Along the road, we have been fortunate to have met wonderful people capable of amazing grace. The best gift my mother ever gave was to introduce us to Deb and

Bob Sterken, with whom we collaborated to establish Friendship House! The next person along our personal journey was an energetic and creative preschool "wizard", who couldn't have embraced Seth and the challenges he brought any more wonderfully if he were her own. The road through public school was made easier because we were fortunate to have a superintendent who "got it" and brought with him one swell special education director who began when Seth entered kindergarten and retired the year he graduated from high school. She gave us Seth's mentor for seven years who continues to be involved in Seth's life, taking him out from time to time and providing professional consultation to Friendship House. Another terribly important person in Seth's journey has been a friend we met through Special Olympics basketball who helped get Seth set up with his employment at New Holland Brewing, a placement that has been one of the most significant in Seth's life.

Where our "story" moves next is uncertain. We wait to see who Seth becomes and what his life requires. We wait to see who and what is available to find solutions at that time. And then we will get to work. When my husband and I are not able to help, I am certain my sons will embrace Seth and his situation. I am hopeful that they have learned from my efforts and will be able to carry the gauntlet on their own, not just benefiting Seth, but anyone else who has similar needs.

WHERE HAVE YOU SEEN GOD IN THIS JOURNEY?
That's a tough one. I feel God in Seth and the courageous and enthusiastic way in which he faces every day, but then, I feel God in each one of my kids. I feel God in every person who steps up to the plate but then, I feel God in the person who sits idle. I feel God in my husband, Rich, who has taught me so many things about dreaming and negotiating, but then, I feel God in those who aren't as forward-looking. I feel God in myself when

I am able to do whatever it takes to arrive at a workable solution, but then, I feel God in myself when I fail.

At times I get frustrated. I get frustrated with the people who spend their days performing tasks in God's name, but couldn't look at my baby when they encountered him or are now unable to treat him as valuable in the adult world. I get frustrated with the people who tell me God chose me for this because I am somehow better able to cope with it. I get frustrated with the mentality of some who believe "God will provide" and thus sit and wait instead of using their own creativity and intelligence to work to help find solutions. I believe God's work happens through rigorous efforts by humans laboring together.

FROM YOUR STORY WHAT ENCOURAGEMENT WOULD YOU GIVE OTHERS?

Early on in my career as a mother, I learned I couldn't realize my dream of changing the institutional world for all kids but I could change it for my kids and in so doing I could help those changes gain momentum. I've learned that it is absolutely necessary to understand the laws that support my position as well as the constraints of the actual system. I have learned that it is my responsibility to figure out how to couch my request in a "win-win" solution for all stakeholders. I've learned that negotiation skills and patience are of utmost importance. There is always another point of view and another option to consider.

I've learned that though I am a shy person uncomfortable with seeking people out, I can put a warm smile on my face and make myself plow through any doorway. The name of the game is courage.

Most importantly, I've learned that passion for the dream is not only the best motivator, but also a primary selling tool because it comes from the heart. Completion of each task will be driven by love and commitment. Good people will be willing to join in, commit, and work to achieve the dream -if one just believes!

continue the conversation

1. What common themes do you hear in these three stories? In what ways do Pam, George, Debbie, and Kathy embody the principles of integrity, imagination, and improvisation?

2. Pam, George, Debbie and Kathy all talk about facing adversity with faith, belief, and courage. Do these stories inspire you to do the same?

ideas for the road: giving thanks

This week write a note, email, or letter to someone who inspires you. It could be a parent, teacher, mentor, or friend, but share with them how you have seen Christ in their lives. You never know how that will impact some-one's life, or your own.

playlist

"I Saw What I Saw", Tell Me What You Know by Sara Groves

inspiration

living a missional life is to live out how one is
called and sent by God.

chapter 9:
finding your story in
God's story

But in your hearts sanctify Christ as Lord. Always be ready to make your defense to anyone who demands from you an account of the hope that is in you. (1 Peter 3:15)

You are my witnesses, says the Lord, and my servant whom I have chosen, so that you may know and believe me and understand that I am he. Before me no god was formed, nor shall there be any after me. (Isaiah 43:10)

But you will receive power when the Holy Spirit has come upon you; and you will be my witnesses in Jerusalem, in all Judea and Samaria, and to the ends of the earth. (Acts 1:8)

THE END?

And so we come to the end of this book, but not the end of the story nor the end of the road. We believe in the living word and the living God. In fact, the place we will meet Jesus again is on the road and along the journey. As we have travelled together, we hope that you have been encouraged by the missional conversation. That in God's story, you have found a center and plotline to your story. That in the conversation, you have been encouraged to live with integrity even in the tension of life. That you have opened yourself to the still small voice which calls us to a missional imagination transcending our current reality. And, that as you go on your way, you have been encouraged to live a life of improvisation trusting in an incarnational God.

While the principles of integrity, imagination, and improvisation are metaphorical, the stories of George, Pam, Debbie, and Kathy put flesh and bones on these ideas. Their stories witness to the power and possibility of the missional life. All of them faced tensions that defied easy answers and yet, within community, they persevered. We hope that they inspire you in your journey.

The root word for inspiration comes from the word spirit and the Latin spiritus, which means "soul, courage, vigor, breath." It is related to spirare, "to breathe."[38] Part of how we live a missional life is a radical opening to the spirit, which does indeed take courage. The journey can begin in many ways, but especially by breathing in the ideas of integrity, imagination, and improvisation. As you journey down the road it may not be about doing more, but it is about integrating these ideas into your life and seeing what God will show you.

Our hope is that this book is an invitation, not because it gives easy answers, but because it challenges you to ask more questions. After beginning this journey into the missional life, you may still feel unsure about your call. You may still be searching for answers. We encourage you to accept the reality of ambiguity and yet adopt an open posture toward God, finding abundant life by trusting God's promises.

For many of us it would be so easy to become cynical,

---

[38] *Online Etymology Dictionary*. Web. 28 Sept. 2011. <http://www.etymonline.com>.

closed-off or too busy, but God calls us to be open. This openness is most profoundly embodied by Christ on the cross whose arms are left wide open to the world. Our challenge is be open to the Spirit which challenges us to see, hear, and respond to the mission of God. Are your arms and hearts open?

THE UNFOLDING STORY

One of the most powerful experiences that Ellen and I (John) have had teaching a class on the missional life is to give people the space to compose and speak their stories in a safe and loving environment. They are able to explore what their lives point to. As people have shared, and the conversation has blossomed, we have been inspired, challenged, and encouraged to stand witness to these stories. In our own walks, we try to integrate these practices.

We offer you that same opportunity here. Consider this book a catalyst to review the arc of your life and an invitation in the company of friends to create space to share your story with others. Be encouraged to think about and reveal to another person how your story and God's story have intersected and are intersecting. If you are willing, take a shot at sharing how you feel called and sent into the world as a creative, imaginative, and improvisational agent of God's glory.

So before you leave the road, share your story and look forward to the next leg of the journey!

continue the conversation

1. Has one of the stories here in this book or in your life inspired you? Do you think that story or person shares any of the principles of integrity, imagination, and improvisation?

2. What does your life point to?   Does it point beyond yourself; does it point to God?

ideas for the road
sharing your story

In a small group, Sunday school class, or just with a group of friends, gather together and share your story with one another in light of the ideas we have presented. How have you heard God's call in your life?   Have you heard that still small voice?   Where do you think you are being sent?   We encourage you to first write down your story.   We suggest that it be about two pages long, as this helps to make sure everyone gets a chance to share.

Here are some ideas to get you started:

• Consider how your story at this moment in time intersects with God's story.
• Write a letter to God.
• Write a letter to a friend or family member.
• Share instances when you sensed the particular presence of God, or the haunting absence from God.
• Share times of struggles in your life and/or in your questing.
• Talk about dreams for your life.

playlist

"Strong Enough", The Story of Your Life by Matthew West

about the authors

We share our stories here not as models to emulate but because we believe sharing one's story is an essential part of life. Often the story is shaped first by holy glimpses and then by questions that emerge from the heart.

john's story

PUT YOUR NAME IN THE PLATE?
I start my story not from the beginning but with a question Tony Campolo, a nationally known minister, once asked in a sermon at Duke Chapel when I was 16 years old. He asked the congregation, "Do you want titles or testimonies in your life?" He asked the crowd, "Do you want more money, more stuff, more power or are you looking to live a meaningful life? A life filled with testimonies of grace, love, and service." In the sermon, not only did Campolo challenge what I believed about faith, he called me to action.

That call to action occurred when he challenged any of the youth and students in the congregation to put their name in the offering plate in order to spend a summer working in inner city Camden, New Jersey. This sermon touched a truth in my soul. It reinforced to me that faith is not just a belief system but it is also a way of life. What was so interesting is that as I sat in that pew, I remember being too scared to risk. I was comfortable. I had my plans for the summer and I was too scared to put my name in that offering plate. I still remember how I felt and how nervous I was. Now, I recognize that I was too comfortable to stretch myself.

A CALL TO INTEGRITY: IS THERE SOMETHING MORE?

Fast forward a number of years. I was 26, living in Charlotte, North Carolina. I had graduated from a good university, I had a good job. In the four years that I had been working, I had tripled my initial salary but there were some lingering questions in my life. Was I practicing what I believed? I said I was a Christian, but was I living that out?

The answer for me was that God was calling me to something more. I was good at what I was doing but there was still a deep sense of longing for meaning. I looked at the partners in our firm and I wondered if the work provided meaning. I wanted my life to mean something. I wanted it to have a larger purpose. I began exploring my gifts and tried to get a sense of God's call. These questions guided my journey, and I decided to attend seminary.

MAKING CONNECTIONS: A MISSIONAL GOD

This sense of call (although I would not have named it as such at the time) led me to a seminary class which focused on a theologian named Lesslie Newbigin. In his work, Newbigin talks about the Missio Dei which is the belief in a missionary God. A God who is working to reconcile God's creation by sending. [39] It is the belief that God the Father sent the Son, and God the Father and the Son sent the Spirit, and now Father, Son and Holy Spirit send the church into the world. We believe in this God who calls ordinary people like you and me and

---

[39] Newbigin, Lesslie. *Trinitarian Doctrine for Today's Mission*. Eugene, OR: Wipf & Stock, 2006. Print. As well as David Bosch shares this idea in Bosch, David Jacobus. *Transforming Mission: Paradigm Shifts in Theology of Mission*. Maryknoll, NY: Orbis, 1991. Print.

sends them into the world to be a part of God's reconciling work. We believe in a God who calls and sends. For me, this was the connection that I had felt that day in Duke Chapel. This was the hungering that I had in my soul to be a part of God's reconciling work in the world. Now, I knew if I was open to God's call, if I was willing to risk, my life could be a part of God's mission in the world. In this understanding of God, I have found meaning in my life. In this understanding of God, I have found what I long for. In this understanding of God, I have heard an invitation to abundant life.

ellen's story

SEARCHING

My "is there more" moment came later in life, after time spent in career, and motherhood, when I found it impossible to ignore the question: *what is God calling me to do?* Such exploration lead to a bigger question: **who does God call me to be?** I felt a nudge, a pull, but toward what? Even when buried under the more pressing needs of each day and, at times, a mental lethargy lending itself to a cycle of numb living, the pull remained persistent. Eventually my soul was taut with the burden of it. Slowly, I began to pour it out through prayer and writing, and conversations with family and friends. I continued to wrestle with the struggle to gain clarity regarding the work in the world to which God called me. I was faced with the concern: If I am not certain of the specific work to which God calls, do I let this ambiguity paralyze me; do I become overwhelmed by drudgery, or blind to possibilities? I began to craft a response, that, in all things, God's purpose will prevail. In all things, God calls me to love God and neighbor. In all things, God calls me to be authentic to God's creation and mission by living as a witness to God's blessing. I trust that God knows me, yearnings and fears included, and calls me anyway by inviting me to step into the work God is already doing. I believe a faithful response to God's call is to trust God to know, plan, and participate in my journey, to be confident of God's love and providence, and to open my life to God.

MEANING

In stepping out in faith, I realized I was setting upon a new course where I had dared not go. My strong preference is for solid ground; and yet I found myself in unchartered waters. Having no desire to sink, I fashioned a metaphorical life boat, built of assurance of God's presence, encouragement of others, and an unfurled heart. I felt the sun's warmth and the wind's insistence in new ways. I looked upon the opaque sea with a little less trepidation. As I began this part of the journey, I became aware that I was foraying into the unknown. I was not taking faith for granted but was exploring it, and my place in the world. Drifting through a variety of weather in this vessel, I became conscious of a burgeoning sensation, somewhat unfamiliar, and I worked to name it: Hope. By God's grace, along the way I am realizing that faith is meant to be aired out! I have become aware that, in the search for meaning, I have found meaning in the searching.

A LIFE-GIVING OPPORTUNITY

Being invited to work on this project has proved to be a life-giving opportunity for me. As mother to three children, I certainly welcome a diversion from the quotidian existence; yet I suspect my desire to write about the missional life goes beyond a mere escape from vacuuming and food preparation! Why is that? It must be that this book addresses my own longing: to consider that I am truly called by God; to embrace the questions of life; to see God in the searching; to serve God in relationship with others; to be content with my "daily bread," and yet to not be complacent with the way things are. Ultimately, my search is to be deeply filled with the "more." The missional journey—listening and responding to God's call—indeed offers "something more" although the "more" is perhaps not what we would expect. I believe God takes the "more" and makes a place. Pulling here, pushing there, enlarging, subtracting, until we know so deeply in ourselves the place where God's holy image has made an impression, where our true self now resides, and we embark upon a life of intentional dialogue with God. I hope, in your encounter with the missional life, God will grow your dwelling place and that you will find the "more" you have been searching for, wishing for, praying for. I hope that we will glorify God by joining our journeys together, all the better to see and hear our God. God speaks our name and calls us from dust to new life. Thanks be to God, who has prepared the way!

resources for the journey

spiritual disciplines

Be still, and know that I am God. (Psalm 46:10a)

THE WHAT AND WHY OF SPIRITUAL DISCIPLINE

Living a missional life means creating space to hear God's call. A spiritual discipline, or practice, may be best understood as making a place in one's life to experience the presence of God.

Christian practices are not activities we do to make something spiritual happen in our lives. Nor are they duties we undertake to be obedient to God. Rather they are patterns of communal action that create openings in our lives where the grace, mercy, and presence of God may be made known to us. They are places where the power of God is experienced. In the end, these are not ultimately our practices but forms of participation in the practice of God.[40]

---

[40] Bass, Dorothy C. *Practicing Our Faith: a Way of Life for a Searching People*. San Francisco, CA: Jossey-Bass, 1997. Print.

William Willimon writes:

> God in Christ takes time for us and interrupts us, throughout the day, if we have the eyes of faith to see it. God takes time from us. God does not wait for us to fine-tune the spiritual disciplines. God grants us the freedom to be about our vocations in the world, doing what we have to do in this life. Then God suddenly shows up, unexpectedly becomes an event in our time, disrupts our lives. While we are busy planning a wedding, God interrupts, impregnates and enlists a young woman in a revolution (Luke 2)... The true God can never be known through our practices but comes to us only as a gift of God, only as revelation. Our practice of the faith is something that God does for us, in us, [and] often despite us.[41]

We do not believe that Christianity itself is a "practice" or that following a spiritual practice is "required" for a faithful walk with God. However, we do believe that spiritual discipline is one way to understand discipleship. Rather than deflect our attention from the living God, the purpose of spiritual discipline is to direct our attention -all our listening ears- toward God. It is an invitation to open the door of our lives, to set aside our plans, to clear our vision in order to meet the God who takes time for us.

INVITATION TO SPIRITUAL DISCIPLINE
Many Christians have found that the intentional making room to meet God through spiritual discipline illumines the faith journey and deepens the walk of discipleship. There are many ways of discipline, some of which are

---

[41] Willimon, William. "Too Much Practice: Second Thoughts on a Theological Movement." *The Christian Century*. 9 Mar. 2010. Web. 26 Aug. 2010. <http://www.christiancentury.org/article.lasso?id=8270>.

listed below. An important guiding question is: is God is being served through this practice? We encourage you to consider these suggestions and to try one—making adjustments as you are inclined- and to be creative in your questing to meet God and hear God's call to you.

Sabbath: a time wholly set apart for the purpose of opening our hearts to God. "To act as if the world cannot get along without our work for one day in seven is a startling display of pride that denies the sufficiency of our generous maker."[42] Set aside a day where you do not work—don't check work email, do turn off the blackberry, etc. Rest, change the rhythm of your life, be at peace.

Daily Office/ Devotional: making time in your day (early morning, evening, in the car -whatever is the best fit for you) to reflect upon God's Word. This time may also be understood as an intentional listening for God. Many devotional resources are available, including online.

Examen: a time of prayer and reflection which invites us to sift through the experiences of our daily life in order to learn from them. Examen is an exercise in discernment which can lead to a realization of God's presence with us in all things.
> "Awareness of what genuinely gives us life (and what deadens that life) will help us to make choices consistent with the work of the Holy Spirit in our lives." (Kris Haig)

Journaling: a written conversation with God, often begun with a seed phrase such as:
> Blessings for which I am grateful...
> Spiritual role models and mentors...

---

[42] Bass, Dorothy C. *Receiving the Day: Christian Practices for Opening the Gift of Time*. San Francisco: Jossey-Bass, 2000. Print.

Persons for whom I want to pray...
Situations for which I want to pray...
Discernment questions...
Scripture I want to read or read again
Questions about faith...
Doubts or worries I wish to give to God...

Fasting: to remove something from the normal regimen of living, often to abstain from food for a designated time. The Presbyterian Church (USA) upholds the historic Christian practice of fasting, for the purpose of prayer, reconciliation, and opening ourselves to God's leading. By fasting, people hope to become closer to God and to be changed. Fasting, in conjunction with prayer, may help us slow down and think about our response to the problems in our world. One opportunity is to join with Presbyterians around the country in a monthly 40-hour fast to help discern ways to respond to the Global Food Crisis (see PCUSA website for additional information).

SPIRITUAL DISCIPLINE RESOURCES
If you are interested in additional reading and/or information, we encourage you to investigate these resources.

Printed material:
Buechner, Frederick. *Now and Then*. [San Francisco, Calif.]: HarperSanFrancisco, 1991. Print.

Dewar, Francis. *Invitations: God's Calling for Everyone : Stories and Quotations to Illuminate a Journey*. London: SPCK, 1996. Print.

Dewar, Francis. *Live for a Change*. N.p.: Darton, Longman & Todd, 1988. Print.

Linn, Dennis, Sheila Fabricant. Linn, and Matthew Linn. *Sleeping with Bread: Holding What Gives You Life.* Mahwah: Paulist, 1995. Print.

Tickle, Phyllis. *The Divine Hours.* Oxford: Oxford UP, 2007. Print.

Winner, Lauren F. *Mudhouse Sabbath.* Brewster, MA: Paraclete, 2003. Print.

Web resources:
http://www.d365.org/todaysdevotion/ (Devotional material)
http://www.inward/outward.org ("Marks of Call" list, Church of the Savior in Washington DC)
http://www.pcusa.org/devotions/ (Devotional material)
http://www.pcusa.org/spiritualformation (Spiritual disciplines)
http://www.pcusa.org/foodcrisis/ (Fasting)

join the conversation

Our hope is that this conversation will go beyond the book.   For additional resources and to add your voice please visit:

www.calledtolife.net

)

bibliography

Bass, Dorothy C. *Practicing Our Faith: a Way of Life for a Searching People.* San Francisco, CA: Jossey-Bass, 1997. Print.

Bass, Dorothy C. *Receiving the Day: Christian Practices for Opening the Gift of Time.* San Francisco: Jossey-Bass, 2000. Print.

Bauckham, Richard. *Bible and Mission: Christian Witness in a Postmodern World.* Grand Rapids, MI: Baker Academic, 2003. Print.

Bosch, David Jacobus. *Transforming Mission: Paradigm Shifts in Theology of Mission.* Maryknoll, NY: Orbis, 1991. Print.

Brooks, David. "The Great Seduction." The New York Times - Breaking News, World News & Multimedia. 10 June 2008. Web. 26 Aug. 2010. <http://www.nytimes.com/2008/06/10/opinion/10brooks.html>.

Buechner, Frederick. *Now and Then.* [San Francisco, Calif.]: HarperSanFrancisco, 1991. Print.

Buechner, Frederick. *Wishful Thinking; a Theological ABC.* New York: Harper & Row, 1973. Print.

Calvin, Jean. *Institutes of the Christian Religion.* Philadelphia: Westminster, 1960. Print.

Chan, Francis, and Danae Yankoski. *Crazy Love: Over whelmed by a Relentless God.* Colorado Springs, CO: David C. Cook, 2008. Print.

Crouch, Andy. *Culture Making: Recovering Our Creative Calling.* Downers Grove, IL: IVP, 2008. Print.

Dewar, Francis. *Invitations: God's Calling for Everyone : Stories and Quotations to Illuminate a Journey.* London: SPCK, 1996. Print.

Dewar, Francis. *Live for a Change.* N.p.: Darton, Longman & Todd, 1988. Print.

Dupree, Janet Rae. "The New York Times Log In." *The New York Times - Breaking News, World News & Multimedia.* 4 May 2008. Web. 26 Aug. 2010. <http://www.nytimes.com/2008/05/04/business/04unbox.html>.

Frost, Michael. *Exiles: Living Missionally in a Post-Christian Culture.* Peabody, MA: Hendrickson, 2006. Print.

Frost, Michael. *Seeing God in the Ordinary: a Theology of the Everyday.* Peabody, MA: Hendrickson, 2000. Print.

George, Sherron Kay. *Called as Partners in Christ's Service: the Practice of God's Mission.* Louisville, KY: Geneva, 2004. Print.

Goetz, David L. *Death by Suburb: How to Keep the Suburbs from Killing Your Soul.* [San Francisco]: HarperSanFrancisco, 2006. Print.

Guder, Darrell L., and Lois Barrett. *Missional Church a Vision for the Sending of the Church in North America.* Grand Rapids, MI: W.B. Eerdmans Pub., 1998. Print.

Guder, Darrell L. *The Continuing Conversion of the Church.* Grand Rapids, MI: W.B. Eerdmans Pub., 2000. Print.

Hall, Ron, Denver Moore, and Lynn Vincent. *Same Kind of Different as Me.* Nashville: Thomas Nelson, 2006. Print.

Heifetz, Ronald A., and Martin Linsky. Leadership on the Line: Staying Alive through the Dangers of Leading. Boston, MA: Harvard Business School, 2002. Print.

Hirsch, Alan. *The Forgotten Ways: Reactivating the Missional Church.* Grand Rapids, MI: Brazos, 2006. Print.

Kilborn, Peter T. "The Five Bedroom, Six-Figure Rootless Life." The New York Times - Breaking News, World News & Multimedia. 1 June 2005. Web. 26 Aug. 2010. <http://www.nytimes.com/2005/06/01/national/class/01ALPHARETTA-FINAL.html>.

Lewis, C. S. *The Four Loves.* New York: Harcourt, Brace, 1960. Print.

Lindvall, Michael L. *A Geography of God: Exploring the Christian Journey.* Louisville, KY: Westminster John Knox, 2007. Print.

Linn, Dennis, Sheila Fabricant. Linn, and Matthew Linn. *Sleeping with Bread: Holding What Gives You Life.* Mahwah: Paulist, 1995. Print.

Tickle, Phyllis. *The Divine Hours.* Oxford: Oxford UP, 2007. Print.

Winner, Lauren F. *Mudhouse Sabbath.* Brewster, MA: Paraclete, 2003. Print.

Livermore, David A. *Serving with Eyes Wide Open: Doing Short-term Missions with Cultural Intelligence.* Grand Rapids, MI: Baker, 2006. Print.

Mahan, Brian. *Forgetting Ourselves on Purpose: Vocation and the Ethics of Ambition.* San Francisco, CA: Jossey-Bass, 2002. Print.

McNeal, Reggie. *Missional Renaissance: Changing the Scorecard for the Church.* San Francisco, CA: Jossey-Bass, 2009. Print.

Merton, Thomas. *My Argument with the Gestapo; a Macaronic Journal.* Garden City, NY: Doubleday, 1969. Print.

Merton, Thomas. *No Man Is an Island.* New York: Harcourt, Brace, 1955. Print.

Moehringer, J. R. *The Tender Bar: A Memoir.* New York: Hyperion, 2005. Print.

Newbigin, Lesslie. *The Gospel in a Pluralist Society.* Grand Rapids, MI: W.B. Eerdmans, 1989. Print.

Newbigin, Lesslie. *The Open Secret: an Introduction to the Theology of Mission.* Grand Rapids, MI: W.B. Eerdmans, 1995. Print.

Newbigin, Lesslie. *Trinitarian Doctrine for Today's Mission.* Eugene, OR: Wipf & Stock, 2006. Print.

Peterson, Eugene H. *Under the Unpredictable Plant: an Exploration in Vocational Holiness.* Grand Rapids, MI: W.B. Eerdmans, 1994. Print.

Placher, William C. *Callings: Twenty Centuries of Christian Wisdom on Vocation.* Grand Rapids, MI: W.B. Eerdmans Pub., 2005. Print.

Putnam, Robert D. *Bowling Alone: The Collapse and Revival of American Community.* New York: Simon & Schuster, 2000. Print.

Rienstra, Debra. *So Much More: an Invitation to Christian Spirituality.* San Francisco: Jossey-Bass, 2005. Print.

Robinson, Anthony B. *Transforming Congregational Culture.* Grand Rapids, MI: W.B. Eerdmans Pub., 2003. Print.

Schultze, Quentin J. *Dancing in the Dark: Youth, Popular Culture, and the Electronic Media.* Grand Rapids, MI: W.B. Eerdmans Pub., 1991. Print.

Schwehn, Mark R., and Dorothy C. Bass. *Leading Lives That Matter: What We Should Do and Who We Should Be.* Grand Rapids, MI: W.B. Eerdmans Pub., 2006. Print.

Wells, Samuel. *Improvisation: the Drama of Christian Ethics.* Grand Rapids, MI: Brazos, 2004. Print.

Willimon, William. "Too Much Practice: Second Thoughts on a Theological Movement." The Christian Century. 9 Mar. 2010. Web. 26 Aug. 2010. <http://www.christiancentury.org/article.lasso?id=8270>.

Made in the USA
Middletown, DE
26 November 2016